ALLIED COMBAT MEDALS
OF
WORLD WAR 2

ALLIED COMBAT MEDALS
OF
WORLD WAR 2

Volume 1: Britain, the Commonwealth and Western European nations

Christopher Ailsby

Patrick Stephens Limited

Dedication
To Lynne, with grateful thanks for all
her help and patience in my collecting
habit, and without whose help none of
my books could have been written.

First published in 1989

*British Library Cataloguing in
Publication Data*
Allied combat medals of World War 2.
    Vol. 1: Britain, the Commonwealth
    and western nations
    1. World War, 1939-1945 — Medals
    2. Armies — Medals, badges,
    decorations, etc. — History — 20th
    century
    940.54′6   D796

    ISBN 0-85059-927-X

Patrick Stephens is part of the Thorsons
Publishing Group

**Printed in Great Britain at
The Bath Press, Avon**

10 9 8 7 6 5 4 3 2 1

Acknowledgements
Grateful thanks to Andrew Litherland,
Josef Charita, Adrian Forman, Albert
Flipts, Lt-Col. (retd.) J. R. Angolia, F. J.
Stephens, Margaret Nobbs, James
Cross, Herbert Spiller, Simon Norris,
Mrs Wendy Jackson, Geoff Wollerton,
Roland Maddocks. Special thanks to
Mrs Pearl Beday for her assistance in
proof-reading and indexing.

Picture credits:
Charita, Josef, *108, 127, 130, 131, 134,
    137, 139, 141, 142, 144, 149, 177,
    178, 179, 180, 181, 196, 214, 215,
    216, 219, 222, 223, 224, 225, 228,
    233, 236, 237, 238, 239*
Cross, James, *105, 111*
Flipts, Albert, *105, 111*
Forman, A., *175, 176, 181, 182, 184,
    186, 187, 189, 240*
Nobbs, Margaret, *65, 66, 67, 68, 73,
    74, 75, 76, 77, 78, 79, 80, 81, 82, 83*
Norris, Simon, *102, 105*
Spink & Son Ltd., *33, 34, 35, 37, 42,
    43, 57, 90, 91, 93, 94, 95, 101, 106,
    107, 108, 110, 114, 117, 121, 122,
    130, 138, 140, 141, 142, 143, 147,
    164, 169, 170, 173, 174, 177, 178,
    180, 181, 192, 193, 194, 195, 197,
    198, 214, 226, 227, 230*
Stephens, Fred, *85*

Contents

Introduction

The First World War culminated in an uneasy peace and political stresses in Europe which could not easily be overcome. Russia had sustained a severe defeat: the serfdom that the Russian people had endured under the Czar, coupled with the horrific deaths on the battlefield and the apparent disregard for human life shown by Russian generals, had produced the catalyst invoking the human response that erupted in 1917 as the Bolshevik revolution. The Germans had used the revolution to obtain Russia's withdrawal from the First World War. The new Communist government removed the Czar and his family by execution, which incensed King George V and the future Edward VIII, for George V and Czar Nicholas were cousins and very close. The Soviet government was then engaged in fighting the White Russians who, to a limited extent, were supported by men and munitions from Great Britain. This support led to an enduring mistrust of Britain in the Soviet Union which still prevails. Germany had been dismembered, as had the Austro-Hungarian Empire, while the Ottoman Empire had just collapsed. 'Johnny Turk' had been considered the sick man of Europe for some considerable time and Britain's aspirations in that area had now come to fruition. Britain played no small part in the establishment of the Arab kingdoms, and the prize of black gold which the Royal Navy so dearly needed had been delivered up through various treaties.

War reparations were meted out on Germany and she was occupied. France, Germany's old enemy, saw this as a glowing opportunity to redress the defeats of the Franco-Prussian War. She savagely interpreted her war reparations and this engendered strong hatred in the Germans, to such an extent that martyrs were eventually to be created to the National Socialist cause. One example is that of a man who probably would otherwise have slipped unnoticed into the pages of history, taking up but the smallest notation (and that would only be as some petty criminal or vandal), but he became the rallying call for the disgruntled. Albert Leo Schlageter, who had fought in the First World War, afterwards became a member of the various Freikorps organizations which then abounded and which were desperately fighting for homelands which had been dismembered and unceremoniously shuffled into the new countries that the Treaty of Versailles had produced. Winston Churchill, at a later date when appeasement was being discussed, retorted, 'How can a country with such a funny name as Czechoslovakia be expected to survive?'

Schlageter took an active part in Freikorps activities and saw action in the Baltic and Upper Silesian regions. Following the French occupation of the Ruhr in 1922 to enforce their demands for war reparation, Schlageter joined the Nazi Party and actively engaged in sabotage against the French. He was caught by the French authorities after blowing up a bridge on 15 March 1923, found guilty and executed by firing squad on 26 May the same year. He became a rallying point for the discontent that was evolving in Germany, exacerbated by the raging inflation which was rampant at the time. (It is interesting to note that during his own trial, Claus Barbie told his defence lawyer that he found himself in the same position on the apprehension of Jean Moulins in Lyons, and that by executing him he had transposed Moulins to the position Schlageter occupied all those years before. Barbie felt that he was mirroring the French executioner of Schlageter.)

Great Britain was also going through a period of economic depression. The late 1920s and early '30s saw the Jarrow hunger marches as well as the discontent of a great number of ex-soldiers who had nowhere to go and plenty of time on their hands. George V and his son, later Edward VIII, shared considerable worries as to the future of the

existence of a democratic monarchy in Great Britain. The rise of socialism and the unions looked as though they would change the face of Britain irrevocably. This situation spawned, through Oswald Mosely, the British Union of Fascists, dedicated to the setting up of a mirror image state to that of Mussolini and his blackshirts in Italy. To this backdrop the country went through a period of appeasement and a running-down of her armed forces.

The United States retreated into a policy of isolationism, which was to keep America out of the Second World War until the inevitable attack on herself. The old ally, Italy, who had out of the treaty of 1919 gained actual territorial acquisitions from the dismembered Austria, had become Fascist. Mussolini was ruling the country under the guise of a democratic monarchy, headed by Victor Emmanuel, a state of affairs which Mosely and the British Union of Fascists took as their model and their goal.

Czechoslovakia, that artificial state whose inhabitants included Czechs, Slovaks, Germans, Magyars and Ukrainians, was full of intrigue. The pro-Nazi, Konrad Henlein, was trying through the auspices and cover of a gymnastic and sports organization, the Turnverband, to amalgamate the Sudetenland with the ill-fated Weimar Republic. The Republic was actively training the members of that organization in military matters, with the hope of annexation. Hitler was to reap the fruits of this movement in later years and claim it as his idea, when in fact he had only inherited the legacy of it from others. Hitler was the great exponent of the absorption of others' ideas which could be regurgitated as his own; he certainly borrowed from Mussolini, who had originally been his mentor with Hitler being the junior partner in Fascism in Europe. In fact during the mid-1930s Hitler was considered by many people preferable and less dangerous than Mussolini. Then the Spanish Civil War erupted in 1936 and the writing was on the wall for the future conflict. Chamberlain, the arch appeaser, returned in 1938 from Munich with the immortal words, 'Peace in our time'. With the conclusion of the Spanish Civil War in March 1939, Spain had been added to the Fascist map of Europe and Hitler had become the undisputed demigod of European Fascism.

The years following the First World War constituted a period of agitated calm that subsequently haemorrhaged into the Second World War. Some historians consider this conflict to be nothing but the conclusion of the First World War and the intervening years between them as, not a peace but a flimsy truce, allowing the realigning of political thought and regrouping by the protagonists into new belligerent states. Those new states formed out of the 1919 peace treaty aligned with the established ones, and produced cohorts that eventually fought on both the Allied and Axis sides.

The general introduction to the build-up of the German armed forces is covered, along with the awards of the orders, medals, badges and decorations of Nazi Germany, in my earlier book *Combat Medals of the Third Reich*. This second volume covers those awards relevant to the European theatre that were bestowed by Britain and those of her allies stationed in Great Britain, as well as those awards to the armies that were raised in occupied Europe, such as the Maquis, with the exceptions of Poland and Czechoslovakia. Poland has been excluded because the government in exile in Britain never really became the operational or effective government of the country at the culmination of the war. Czechoslovakia is also excluded because, although the country experienced a brief spell of post-war independence, it soon fell to Soviet machinations. Thus these two nations, alongside the Soviet Union and the United States of America, will be covered in a subsequent volume on Allied combat awards.

I would, at this point, like to thank those who have received *Combat Medals of the Third Reich* so well and the great number of people who have taken the time to write and give information.

However, one source of criticism has been levelled that I did not list all my sources for the research. These sources, I would like to make clear, will be detailed in the large, three-volumed work presently underway, in conjunction with David Littlejohn and John R. Angolia. This, I thought, had been explained in the foreword of the book by Jack: 'However, in this case, it serves merely as an introduction to a future work planned by the author, as well as an introduction to the author himself.' Likewise, I have not listed the sources for this book, as it is possible that this book also may be enlarged and it would be at that point that this would be implemented. In conjunction with this, I will list the sources of acquisition of the actual pieces, to enhance pedigree of the items – for it has also been claimed, 'Many illustrations of known copies and fakes, which new collectors or dealers will assume to be original pre-1945. Fortunately, experienced collectors and dealers will know better!'

I have never wanted to lend authenticity to bogus items and have made every attempt to correct any inadvertent mistakes, to which ends I removed the Alpers document from the reprint after receiving proof positive of its sordid past from advanced collector Arthur W. Charlton. In an excellent article in *Info* by Jörg-M. Hormann, on the Cross of Honour for the Relatives of the Dead in Spain, he cites the medal on page 29 as a copy. Albeit that it is not like the copies he describes, another authentic piece has been acquired and will be substituted, if possible, in the next reprint. The rest of the medals illustrated that are not credited to their respective owners are in my own collection, of which, I am happy to say, 90 per cent were purchased from Adrian Forman of Shepherd Market, London, and are available for scrutiny by the serious historical researcher. I can only reiterate my comment that a piece must be handled to know its authenticity, for even great experts can get it wrong from photographs. Dr. Klietmann commented in a critique about the photographs on page 71, 'page 71 – copy'. In fact, this was an obverse and reverse of two pieces, of which both are without doubt original, the Pössl

piece having been returned to his widow in 1944 by the German army and the other having been purchased from Adrian, who subsequently repurchased it and sold it to another collector with pedigree from the book. The good doctor subsequently wrote to me after I had forwarded him the relevant information, saying one could not be sure without actually handling the piece.

The important fact that these points bring forward, is that it stimulates debate which must lead to a better understanding of the hobby. It is always very pleasant to receive the accolades, but one must also receive the criticisms and try and answer them to the betterment of the collecting fraternity.

I hope this book will give the reader much pleasure and be a source through which to research their medal collections, and that it will stimulate readers to comment through their knowledge and provide a greater input to further books. It is hoped that German political and civilian awards and those of the foreign volunteers and puppet states that were aligned with Germany will also be covered in a future volume. I would once again ask you, the reader, to communicate any information or interesting items you have in your collection for use in future books. I would also like to ask any reader who knows the present whereabouts of the Territorial Efficiency Medal (GB.D028) awarded to Sgt. A. G. Mears MM, no. 1459584, to contact the author.

A brief description of the method of cataloguing is placed below. The individual country is represented by a

code which is added to the individual
type of award.

Awards

Air Force	—	A
Army	—	a
Clasp	—	C
Decorations	—	D
Navy	—	N

Countries

Belgium	—	BE
Commonwealth	—	CM
Denmark	—	DN
France	—	FR
Great Britain	—	GB
Holland	—	NE
Norway	—	NW

An overview of collecting

The question I am most frequently asked is 'What do you collect?', followed by 'Why?', and then sometimes by 'Surely that's a load of old rubbish?' or 'Aren't you glorifying war?' The first question is the easiest to answer and will be self-evident to readers of this book. The second is trickier and I will return to it in a moment. The third is also easy: decorations which involve the artistry and craftsmanship of the finest jewellers in the world cannot be called 'rubbish'. The last question is harder. It is certainly not my intention in any way to glorify war, but medals do reward and commemorate acts of valour and collecting them can rapidly become an obsession. For the serious collector this leads to meeting many interesting people, some of whom become life-long friends. Then there is also the thrill of the chase.

I am sure most collectors have had the experience of being told of an item that they had always dearly loved, and that moment of realization when the prized object is obtained. Sometimes you have the exhilaration of the rare opportunity of experiencing history in the making at first hand as well as stimulating the interest of others in the subject. The latter I find

particularly rewarding and can illustrate by the case of Wendy Jackson. Her father, Squadron Leader Fox, had been killed in action before she was born. She had known little of him as her mother had remarried and her closeness as a young girl with her father's family had been a little strained.

She and her mother ventured into our chemist's shop one day having learned of my interest in medals, and offered me his DFM. As usual I asked if there was anything to go with it. They said they had photos, a print signed by the artist, Salisbury, in which her father was the pilot and an oil painting of him in his flying helmet. They were slightly bemused that I would be even interested in these old relics. A deal was struck and they assured me of their help in putting together the information on him and his crew.

At this point, I must stress a real collector gets good 'vibes' and I had the strangest feeling of the medal trying to tell its story. The events around the crew in my investigations led me to some unusual experiences. First I traced 'Lofty' Maddocks, a talented artist who had lost the sketch book that he had kept during his captivity upon his return from the forced march from East Prussia that a great number of RAF prisoners had to endure. On contacting him he commented that this was most peculiar as he had not heard of any of the crew or their fate since their plane was hit and he had baled out on the night of 24/25 October 1942 and receiving my letter. Furthermore, four weeks earlier he had received his sketch book, returned by the Canadian government, who had been trying since 1945 to find him, as one of their nationals had picked it up and realized its significance.

The two remaining crew members, one from south London and the other from Liverpool, were far more elusive. Trying the telephone directory and incurring an horrendous phone bill proved fruitless. However, a letter care of the pensions department of the RAF, brought a response. To my great surprise one, Mr Geoff Wollerton, lived in in the same village as my co-director and his children had gone to the same school as my daughters. The other lived only twenty miles away. During the compiling of the story, Fox's daughter became engrossed in the history of her father and she continued the researches on a wider field, to such an extent that we accompanied Mr Wollerton to a village just inside Nottinghamshire to meet 'Dizzy' Spiller. So on Tuesday, 7 April 1987, we witnessed the first meeting of these two men since that night in October 1942 when they had stood in the hatch of the burning Halifax 'D' for Donald and jumped into the night, one to walk into captivity and one to walk out of Europe through

Gibraltar to return to his old squadron at Elsham Wolds three months later with the immortal words, 'Who's moved my kit?'

The participation in history is illustrated by the passages that follow. The description of Fox's wedding, the style of reporting and the list of presents that were given highlight the aspirations of people at that time, and show the shortages that were beginning to bite the general population of Great Britain. This snapshot of the period I hope gives those who did not experience the period at first hand a glimpse of life as it was lived then. You, the reader, could possibly compare the account with write-ups in equivalent papers today and notice the marked change in style and content. Thus, I hope the following accounts show not only this but what can be learned from one small medal, some old photos and a letter, the last vestiges of a young human life snuffed out in battle over some foreign field.

It is hoped that this particular example will show how modern archaeology can unearth not only the autobiographical details and conditions that people lived under in the Second World War but also give a glimpse into the feelings and aspirations of the fighting volunteers of the period. It also demonstrates how one single medal, when it comes into the hands of an experienced collector, can open the doors that have been closed for nearly fifty years.

Sydney Horace Fox was an intellectual man who had trained with a firm of accountants and subsequently joined Barclays Bank. He had been caught up with the war hysteria and the 1930s craze for flying and had enlisted in the Royal Air Force Volunteer Reserve on 20 August 1939, as Aircraftman 2nd Class No 741912. He was promoted the next day, 21 August 1939, to Sergeant and was mobilized on 1 September 1939, remustering as a pilot on 20 May 1940. It was during the early days of the first months of the war when the country needed heroes that men like Sydney took up the challenge and won their decorations. But more of that later, for a strange quirk of circumstance led him to be chosen to be the pilot in the picture 'The Briefing' by Salisbury. He and his crew were also the subject of a number of pictures that were taken for propaganda purposes to inspire a flagging British morale. He was also chosen with his crew, to be used in an RAF calendar, the picture depicting them walking away from a Hampden bomber in flying gear. In 1941 he was the subject of the war artist Blondel for another piece of propaganda art work which gave rise to a fine oil painting of a bomber ace in a flight helmet. He went on to be commissioned to Squadron Leader after his award of the DFM which he received on 11 February 1941 with Sergeant S.R. Gear, No 751359, and Sergeant G.D. Thomas, No 751987. The entry is for gallantry and devotion to duty in execution in air operations.

Fox had been married five months earlier and I have included a beautiful account of the wedding which sets the tone of the period and puts the reader in the mood of the recipient and his family and friends in the sunny days of 1940. 'Two well known

Above *Sydney Fox standing beside his Hawker Hind, wearing the 1930 pattern flying suit. He enlisted as Aircraftman Second Class under training in the RAF Volunteer Reserve on 20 August 1938, and was promoted to Sergeant the next day.*

Woking families were united in the marriage at St Mary's, Horsell, on Saturday, 7 September 1940. Miss Bessy Gwendolyn Bleach, the youngest daughter of Mr and Mrs J. Bleach of 19 Oaks Road, Woking, and Sergeant Sydney Horace Fox, RAF (VR), youngest son of Mr and Mrs J.R. Fox, Turnoak, Wych Hill Lane, Woking. Mr Bleach gave away his

Below *Blondel's painting of Sydney Fox*

daughter, who had three bridesmaids and a page. These were Miss Gladys Fox, sister of the bridegroom, Miss Shirley Marchant, niece of the bridegroom, Miss Joyce Barton, friend of the bride and Master John Knight, nephew of the bride.

'The bride wore a charming dress of French silver net over silk taffeta cut on classic lines with a heart-shaped neckline and having sleeves full to the elbow, with tight cuffs covering the hands. A long embroidered veil was held in place by a spray of white heather. She also wore white crepe de chine sandals and a pearl necklace, and carried a two-way sheaf of Madonna lilies, with sprigs of white heather. The bridesmaids wore ankle length dresses of maize coloured silk lace, over gold silk taffeta slips, with brown velvet sashes, long caps edged with brown velvet, gold crosses and chains, the gifts from the bridegroom and carried shower bouquets of Tea-Roses. The page wore long trousers of brown velvet, with a gold taffeta blouse and a gold tie pin and brown Oliver Cromwell shoes. The best man was Sergeant A.E. Burrows, RAF (VR) and the Groomsmen Messrs A.J. and G.W. Bleach.

Below *Saturday 7 September 1940 saw the tranquil wedding of Syd to Bessy. One year after the declaration of war, England was little changed.*

The curate of St Mary's, the Reverend Richard B.T. Gardner, conducted the service which was fully choral. The choir meeting the bride at the church door and accompanying her down the aisle singing the hymn, "Lead us heavenly father". Other hymns included "Oh perfect love" and "Love divine". Psalm 67 was chanted and accompaniment was provided by Miss Rosemary Newman at the organ who also played the Wedding March.

'A reception attended by seventy guests was held at Turnoak, Woking, the home of the bridegroom's parents. Numerous presents were received including a cut glass cruet from the staff of the Woking Post Office, a canteen of cutlery from the bride's parents and a wireless set from the bridegroom's parents. The bride's gift to the bridegroom was a gold signet ring and the bridegroom's to the bride, a silver fox bolero. After the reception Sergeant and Mrs Fox left for a secret destination, the bride wearing a Marocian dress with the silver fox bolero, black hat, long black kid gloves, shoes and handbag.

'The bride has been employed at the Woking Post Office as a telephonist for six years and before joining the RAF the bridegroom worked for Barclays Bank. Sergeant and Mrs Fox are able to make their home at Lincoln.'

After the wedding Sydney went on to win the DFM and was written up in the local newspaper once again as 'DFM for old Woking flyer, Sergeant S.H. Fox honoured.

'News of another honour which has been conferred on a local flyer was received this week when the

Above *Sydney Fox on the day of the award-ing of his Distinguished Flying Medal (GB.D015). The actual medal and wings are illustrated in the relevant sections of the book.*

announcement of the award of the Distinguished Flying Medal to Sergeant Pilot Sydney Horace Fox, son of Mr and Mrs J.R. Fox, Turnoak, Wych Hill Land, Woking, was made public. He has gained his decoration for distinguished flying, excellent leadership and devotion to duty when flying over Germany and German occupied territory, over a long period.

'Sergeant Pilot Fox is an old boy of the Woking County School. Several awards to former pupils have been previously announced. He came to Woking in 1917 at the age of three years and after leaving school was employed by Messrs Middleton & Tow, Chartered Accountants of London, with whom he remained for some time. Mr Sydney Fox then entered Barclays Bank and had been a

member of their staff for five years, for the latter two of which he devoted his spare time to learning to fly. At the outbreak of the present war he was called up for service as a Sergeant Pilot, in the Bomber Command, and in this capacity he has made many raids over enemy country. These have reached a good number, before his marriage which took place in Horsell in September of last year.'

Following this report Fox wrote to the *News and Mail* and subsequently a report was published under the heading 'Bombing with the RAF, Woking Pilot's anxious five minutes', and goes on to say: 'An interesting letter has been received from Sergeant Pilot S.H. Fox, RAF (VR) (an old Woking County School boy), who as announced in the *News and Mail* on 14 February was recently awarded the Distinguished Flying Medal for meritorious conduct. The circumstances leading up to the decoration have not been announced but Sergeant Pilot Fox has had his full share of perils, calling for coolness and courage of a high order.

'In a letter he writes, "On most of the 28 raids on which I have been, we have been fortunate enough to find and bomb our primary target, our greatest enemy being the weather. On one trip I had no less than $1\frac{1}{2}$ inches of ice inside my cockpit, covering all the instruments and controls, not to mention myself. As we were in ten-tenths clouds at the time I had to get my navigator, whose cockpit was comparatively free, to set pencils, one fore and aft and the other laterally on the table, in order that I might correct any overbanking, climbing or diving whilst I turned to get out of

Above *Squadron Leader Fox (at the time Sergeant) looks over a map in the briefing room of Number 83 Squadron at Scampton, circa February 1941.*

the cloud. I naturally have a great respect for the enemy flak, but do not want to have another anxious five minutes as we experienced that night."'

After this account of flying and his receipt of his decoration, Fox was discharged on appointment to a commission on 4 March 1941 and granted a commission as a Pilot Officer on probation in the general duties branch of the RAF Volunteer Reserve, for the duration of hostilities. Following his promotion he flew only one flight, on 12 March 1941, for which we have no idea of any details, as the records are very sketchy. At this period of time he left the squadron and returned to 14 OTU at Cottesmore in Lincolnshire as an instructor.

He and his wife rented a lovely little cottage in the picturesque village. She related to me that this was a very quiet and restful time in their lives and they remained there until 2 August 1941 when he went to the Central Flying School at Chobham. This was an interesting posting as it

was the base at which he learnt to fly in his early days and is illustrated by the photo of him on p. 13, standing by a Hawker biplane. He remained at this posting until the 23rd of the same month.

On 24 August 1941 he was transferred to 25 OTU at Finningley. Here he was again an instructor. At Finningley he lived on the base and his wife lived at Doncaster. Mrs Fox indicated to me that this was not a period that was particularly edifying to either of them, especially as it was at this time that she found that she was going to have a baby. Her digs and lack of communication with her husband induced her to return home to be with her parents in Woking.

On 13 June 1942 Fox went to 103 Squadron at Elsham Wolds in Lincolnshire, and was promoted on 30 September 1942 to the rank of Squadron Leader. The first flights that he made with the squadron were on the 22nd and 25th of that month, to Emden and Bremen, and were in Wellingtons. He had an aversion to these aircraft and when he converted to Halifaxes told his wife that he considered the Wellingtons dangerous, and that he was delighted to be converted to the new planes.

Sydney took up his administrative duties with gusto. He was well suited to this role and was used to welcome the new crews to the squadron. 103 Squadron had a number of foreign or Dominion crews. They were far from home and Fox's calm but forceful discipline was a reassuring influence on these young men. A wonderful account to this effect is recorded in Don Charlwood's book, *No Moon Tonight*. Charlwood is an Australian and his book is highly regarded and well worth reading as a squadron history. He flew with 103 and gives an in-depth account of flying with Bomber Command during the Second World War, when night after night the bombers were sent out to raid Germany and Italy. It tells of the appalling casualty rates among the crews, of the young men like Fox haunted by the thoughts of death and the loss of comrades, and of terror and anxieties laced with the dangers of flying on missions deep into the heart of enemy territory. It is at this point, through the pages of the book, that we can recall and participate in an eye-witness account of Squadron Leader Fox's grip on the new crews.

'The new crews were sent to the crewroom to await the arrival of the Wing Commander. After half an hour he came but they had not seen him until an indignant voice from behind had addressed the crews sharply, "Don't you stand up when your CO enters the room?" He was a man of perhaps 27 or 28, tall and with a high complexion, higher now than usual with anger. His eyes were blue-grey, his hair receding, he wore an RAF battledress on which were the ribbons of the DSO and DFC. "Tonight there will be no operations." The news appeared to annoy him slightly; but among the men there was a visible relaxing. He went on to say, "Squadron Leader Fox will see the new crews in his room. The rest of you will report here again at 1 o'clock." We were left then with two Squadron Leaders, of whom Fox was evidently the senior. He was compactly built and somehow panther like. His steps were soft and full of

spring, his eyes narrow and gleaming, as though he were keyed always to high pitch. On his head a shapeless ops cap and over his battledress pocket was the ribbon of the DFM. The ribbon commanded their immediate respect. DFMs were seldom given for nothing nor did many Sergeants become Squadron Leaders.

'The second Squadron Leader was Kennard. Besides a DFC he wore two operational adornments, the usual ops cap and a wide moustache. His eyes were dark and staring as though constant peering into darkness had left them so. He was, I believe, little more than a boy and it was sometimes said on the squadron that he wore his moustache to disguise his youth.

'Fox sat casually on the table. "I would like to have a yarn with you chaps who have just come to the squadron. I see that most of you have come from Australia and one or two from Canada. I know that our ideas of discipline are not quite the same as in the colonies." An airman named Geoff rose to his feet. "Excuse me sir, we come from the Dominions." Fox looked at him disconcertedly. "I— Yes, I had fogotten you chaps prefer the term Dominions don't you?" Kennard stared at Geoff with more than intensity as though noting his face for future reference, but from the men there were murmurs of agreement. "In any case", Fox continued in a hardening voice, "discipline among the Sergeants has become very lax, and unless there is a big improvement we shall be obliged to tighten up on privileges."

'A week later Fox addressed the full squadron, bringing unbelievable

Above *This picture was taken in the POW camp in Germany circa 1943, 'Lofty' Maddocks is on the left. The sergeant on the right displays the Navigators' Wing (GB.A006).*

good news. "You will be glad to know that we are to convert shortly to Lancasters." His voice was drowned by an outburst of cheering and shouting. "Next week we take delivery of the first aircraft and will begin a period of intense training. We are the first Squadron in 1 Group to convert and the CO is anxious that we do so as quickly as possible." Fox was most memorable, as he outlined the training scheme. He was still the narrow-eyed, panther-footed Squadron Leader but he was also an enthusiastic boy.'

At this point we must look at one of Fox's crew for details of his last flight, 'Lofty' Maddocks. In correspondence he explains that he lived in Bolton, Lancashire, and had trained as a lithographic artist. He volunteered for the RAF on 4 September 1939 when he was 24. His first posting was to Padgate and on the following day he went to the RAF reception centre, Catterick Bridge. In January 1940 he went for initial flying adaptation. In March 1940 'Lofty' went to navigation school at Bexhill-on-Sea, Sussex. Gunnery,

navigation and initial flying training was undertaken in May 1940 at Pwllheli, North Wales. In July 1940 he went to Aston Down, Gloucester, to number 5 OTU. After the course he was kept on as an instructor. In January 1941 he was transferred with 5 OTU to Church Fenton. In June of that year he transferred to 53 OTU, East Fortune, Scotland, then was posted in April 1942 to number 12 Squadron, Bomber Command, stationed at Binbrook, Lincolnshire. Here he was flying Wellingtons.

Two weeks later 'Lofty' was posted to 103 Squadron at Elsham Wolds. Here a few odd flights were undertaken on Wellingtons, Fox's aversion. These included mine laying over the North Sea and square searches for overdue aircraft. 'Lofty' then converted to Halifax bombers and it was at this point he crewed up with Squadron Leader Fox, as bomb aimer. The rest of the crew were 'Dizzy' Spiller (navigator), Wollerton (wireless operator), Jock Mercer (rear gunner), Tommy Wright (mid-upper gunner) and 'Fitz' Fitzsimmons (engineer). At this juncture in time, the crew collected a brand new 'D' for Donald at Radlett Airfield, Hertfordshire. 'Lofty's' recollections of their flights were Aachen, Duisburg, Dusseldorf, Frankfurt, Mainz, Kassel, Flenburg, Emden, Freiburg and Cologne. He pointed out that he has no log book to verify these flights but in his recollection by 17 October 1942 'D' for Donald was the sole survivor of the original conversion. At this point it is interesting to note and quote from a letter that Fox wrote to his mother and father one Sunday evening.

'Dear Mother and Dad,

'When I rang you up last night I quite thought I had finished work and would be able to write you but no I had to go out again. Tonight I am OC night flying — it's now about quarter to one and things are quiet for a bit so am settling down to write you.

'We had the managing director of a large steel works over to look over the aerodrome one day last week and he invited us — when we had a day of bad weather — to go over to their place to look over the works.

'Going back a bit though, I had to take him out to look over an aircraft and of course showed him 'D' for Donald. Immediately he saw the fox on the side he asked me if I would like him to get me a silver fox, stainless steel fox, for a mascot — of course I didn't say no. Apparently he went back to his works and telephoned the managing director of one of his subsidiary companies, the Silver Fox Steel Co Ltd, and in order to get the mascot for me told him I had called the aircraft "The Silver Fox". Well, Friday was a bad day here as regards weather and as we couldn't do any flying the Wing Commander let us off lectures and we went over to the works. There I found one of each of the following for each member of the crew. A silver fox paper knife, ashtray, bottle opener and pair of cuff links and a letter from the managing director of the firm promising a head of a silver fox in stainless steel, set on an ebony base $10\frac{1}{2}$ inches high, also a smaller one for the aircraft.

'Whilst we were there at the works, this gentleman rang us up to say that all the 4,000 employees of this factory were thrilled about a Halifax named the Silver Fox and that they wanted to adopt the crew. He also wants us to get a 48-hour leave to go over to these works some forty to fifty miles away where we would be "certainly given a right royal welcome" as he put it. It rather looks now as though I shall have to call it the Silver Fox — instead of the Flying Fox — doesn't it?

'Well we looked over the works and afterwards spent the evening with the works home guard, telling them generally about our job. It was most interesting so now I am looking forward to visiting the Silver Fox works in the future. It certainly gave us all a break and was most interesting to see huge blocks and rivers of white hot metal being handled like butter — I will certainly be able to tell you something about it when I come home.'

The last few days are recalled by Lofty in a jaunty fashion and are quite graphic. 'On the Tuesday evening of 20 October 1942 there was a phone call from Wing Commander "Sailor" Malan, previously CO 5 OTU at Sutton Bridge. He asked enquiringly, "Would you like to join a new OTU as an instructor?" I replied, "Thank you very much, yes!" "Sailor" Malan was on the phone on Thursday 22 October to say that the posting was confirmed and on its way.

'On the Friday morning, 23 October, Squadron Leader Fox called me to the flight office. He announced to me that the posting had come through. Fox then stated that from now on you "are off the squadron strength, sorry to lose you".

'I decided to phone my wife in Edinburgh. We had been married for only eight weeks. I wanted her to come down to Barnetby for the weekend. "Sailor" Malan was flying up on Monday morning from Sutton Bridge to Elsham Wolds to collect me. Saturday morning, 24 October, my wife arrived at 9 am at Barnetby. 10 am tannoy for Flight Sergeant Maddocks. The message was abrupt — report to Squadron Leader Fox. I entered Fox's office, he greeted me with, "Operations tonight, would you like to do one more op?" "Where?", was my reply. "Italy" said Fox. "Never seen the Alps before", I replied good humouredly. "Piece of cake", retorted Sydney Fox. "OK", I stated enthusiastically. I was now confined to camp. I phoned my wife to tell her the good news. "See you tomorrow morning at 11 am", I reassuringly informed her.

'The briefing was Target Milan with take-off at 18:30. This was the extreme range for the Halifax and the bomb load was seven 1,000 lb high explosives and four 1,000 lb incendiaries. It was planned to land at Ford, Sussex, on return to refuel. We were due back at Elsham 4 am on Sunday. The route was Dungeness and Etaples, north of Paris, Alps, then Milan, climb to 19,000 ft, drop the bombs and return.'

This was to be one of the last operations on which Halifaxes were used by 103 Squadron. Squadron Leader Fox gathered his crew together for the flight to Milan in their Halifax, number *W1188*. The fuselage was marked with the squadron code *PM* and the call letter *D* for Donald. The crew for the flight that night were Squadron Leader Fox, pilot; Sergeant Henry Frederick Wood No 1383304, second pilot; Warrant Officer Herbert John Spiller, No 580911, navigator; Flight Sergeant Roland Maddocks, No 968023, bomb aimer; Flight Sergeant Norman Alexander Mercer, No 817193, rear gunner; Sergeant Philip Charles Heath, No 1375414, mid-upper gunner; Sergeant Laurence Fitzsimmons, No 617112, flight engineer; and Pilot Officer Geoff Wollerton, No 549093, wireless operator. The unusual point about the crew was that it was made up of eight men instead of the usual seven. The extra man was Wood who had joined the crew as the second pilot, because the long journey to Milan warranted the use of two pilots. This doubling-up system was

Below *Flight Sergeant 'Jock' Mercer*

also used as a method of training less skilful or experienced pilots.

At this point 'Dizzy' Spiller takes up the story. 'In my case, the flight was the last of my second tour of operations, although, had we returned, I may well have carried on to see the rest of the crew through their tours. The time of take off shown in the hours column of the log is a little suspect at 20:00 hours, since the entry was not made out until my return after three months and was purely a guess. In view of the fact that we were brought down at Ligny-Borrois near Nancy, I would now consider it more likely to have been 22:00 hours although Bomber Command flight logs may reveal the actual time. Certainly the flight lasted through the night of 24/25 October 1942.

'The attack, as far as I remember, lasted a very short time. Perhaps one or maybe two passes by a fighter which apparently was a Me 110. There was no prior warning given by the gunners and no word came from them after the attack, and I have assumed that they were killed in the ensuing attack. Tracer bullets entered my position of the aircraft and the port engines appeared to be on fire. I heard the captain give the order to abandon aircraft. I went forward, passing underneath Wood, who had rigged up the second pilot's seat. Fitzsimmons was still at his post at the engineer's panel, but he followed me forward. The captain and Wood were illuminated by the fires and the aircraft was beginning to dive steeply but presumably under Fox's control. Wollerton and Maddocks in the front cabin had by that time donned their

Above *D for Donald, 'The Silver Fox': Squadron Leader Fox's Halifax, drawn in the POW camp by 'Lofty' Maddocks. His impression of the crew just prior to their take-off.*

Below *On the right, 'Dizzy' Spiller; taken at Gibraltar after his escape from occupied Europe. A full account of his exploits is given in his own book,* Ticket to Freedom.

parachutes and were assembled by the escape hatch. This subsequently I learned I had kicked out.

'Wollerton went first. I was a little delayed as I had in my hurry clipped the parachute the wrong way round and this had to be readjusted, so that the ripcord was properly available. Maddocks meanwhile waited for me to go out next, as was the drill. I then left with Maddocks at the hatch and Fitzsimmons behind him. Wollerton was reputedly later to have written to another squadron member from a prison camp to the effect that everyone else had been killed as the aircraft blew up after he had left it. This may well have been the case after Maddocks had baled out. As far as I know Wollerton was picked up pretty quickly. Maddocks will give you his own story. For myself, I was fortunate enough to land and find immediate help, in the form of a hat and a pair of shoes and I walked next day first to Bar-le-Duc and then to St Dizier in the hope of seeing some crew members on the way.

'I eventually made my way to Paris and by diverse means contacted the famous Comete Line and through them made my way to Gibraltar, via Belgium, France and Spain, arriving back in England after three months.'

'Lofty' fills in the other portions of the attack and states that at approximately 21:15 hours just east of Paris he disconnected his intercom and parachute harness 'to go aft to the toilet — uneventful — on the way back to the nose cannon shells and tracers flying past. Put on helmet and intercom, being attacked by fighters from behind, starboard engines on fire, more shells, front perspex

canopy shattered, maps and papers flying all around. Over the intercom Squadron Leader Fox, "Sorry blokes, no control, bale out". Wollerton kicks out the escape hatch and disappears, "Dizzy" Spiller is next to jump out. At this point still trying to fasten my own harness, disconnected for my visit aft. Jump out with one clip out of four not connected, glimpses of flames, parachute opens, in silence, one flash and explosion, swinging mist, wet rain, sick, absolute blackness, where's the ground, nothing, no lights, thump completely winded, finally staggered up, ploughed field, stubble, trees, fifty yards, collect parachute together, staggered through undergrowth down and out. Later, lit a fag, seven Craven A left, roll up in 'chute and sleep.

'Daylight, sound of church bells, bury 'chute after tearing strip for bandage for twisted knee. Get away from here, where to? Obviously south, somewhere east of Paris, make for Switzerland, out of wood nothing in sight. After about half a mile I came to a country road, amazing I encountered a stone milestone, Void 17 kilometres, Toul 29 kilometres. I got out my handkerchief map, position pinpointed, no trouble. After only half an hour I made about three miles across country where I laid up until nightfall. PM — passed through small village which I have since revisited, knocked on the door of a cottage on the outskirts of the village — "Aviateur Anglais" — didn't want to know me. Second day laid up on the edge of a canal and watched the barges go by, regretted it ever since for possibly these barge families may have been friendly. Took off and hit a railway, walked along the sleepers all night. This proved to be slightly awkward, about six inches shorter than my natural stride. No trains, realized lines were rusty, stayed all day in plate layer's hut, again since revisited. Back on the road all night. Encountered no traffic but at 7 am two gendarmes on bikes came out of the blue from round a corner, asked for food as I had had none for four days. Cigs finished, turnips not very filling. Took me to small peasant cottage (prehistoric), woman therein gave me fried egg, cheese, bread. Meantime, one gendarme disappeared to return with one small, fat (obese), garlic smelling inspector, who lost no time in acquainting me with the fact that "Vous êtes prisonnier de guerre".

'The village Demange-aux-Eaux. That was that. One night in the local cell, finding out that Lancashire French is a wee bit removed from the local patrons'. Following morning, German army arrive. One Hauptmann, one Feldwebel, one private second class and very nervous, in a Volkswagen registration number AWH. I can't remember the number but it's a Bolton, Lancs, registration, which I thought was very fitting until I found out that the whole German army was WH. Taken to Bar-le-Duc, on to St Dizier and handed over to the Luftwaffe. Here the pilot of the night fighter, a Me 110, who shot us down, came to see me. Very correct, shades of Richthofen and Hells Angels. "Did I smoke?" A packet of Players, from Dunkirk of course. Finally, I took the train to Frankfurt, on to Main Dulag Luft Airforce

Transit Camp, the first of the prison camps I was to encounter.'

Geoff Wollerton recalls that on the morning of 23 October 1942: 'I was glad to hear we would be on operations that night. I had arranged previously to meet a girlfriend in York on the following afternoon and knew this could now be confirmed as it was unlikely we should be on operations for two nights running.

'The usual flight test and preoperational activity took place. Briefing disclosed Milan as the target which pleased us all as this promised a relaxed, trouble-free flight to and from the target with little opposition round the target itself — and with a pleasant view of the Alps to add a continental holiday flavour to the outing.

'We had flown about 100 hours together as a Halifax crew and so our pre-flight activity provided no problems. My own checks as the wireless operator were confined to ensuring that the radio receiver/transmitter/intercom worked satisfactorily, although no transmissions could be made as we operated in radio silence except in emergency.

'I was rarely called upon for any radio activity as "Dizzy" Spiller was a brilliant navigator; he was a wizard with his sextant when the stars were visible — with GEE* when in range — and DR navigation never let us down to my knowledge; so he made the need for radio as a navigational aid relatively unimportant. I merely needed to check radio beam signals and repractise obtaining loop bear-

* A navigation aid employing ground transmitters and airborne receivers.

ings from friendly or known enemy transmissions. I was keen on keeping in practice with the loop homing devices because if the worst happened and we lost the services of "Dizzy" we could make it back to base using the radio receiver only as a navigational aid. I had been involved in experimental loop homing in 1940 when with 106 Squadron in Hampdens, when I was able to show we could follow and find an aircraft transmitting intermittently on a known frequency. These experimental flights terminated when a Hampden I was following at night at about fifty miles distance flew into the Coventry balloon barrage and crashed, killing all the crew.

'I had already carried out my secondary duty checks of the availability and correct storage of the flares and photo-flashes. I was responsible for dropping these as required — flares for drift sights and illuminations and flashes for target photographs. I was particularly careful about checking the flare chute mechanism as on a recent operation a ten-second photo-flash fuze lit as I pulled out a safety pin. This should have allowed a spinning propeller mechanism to fire a pin into the fuze when the flare dropped clear of the aircraft. Instead it operated immediately. The chute mechanism did not operate correctly to drop the flash and burning fuze out of the tube so I had to lift the photo-flash out of the tube, dash across and open the door (fortunately it opened inwards and so could be opened and closed fairly easily in flight), and throw the offending photo-flash through the open doorway. As the flash did not go off till I had closed the door the adrenalin was

Above *Pilot Officer Geoff Wollerton, here as a sergeant, clearly showing the RAF Air Gunners' Wing (GB.A003).*

obviously working overtime and had speeded up my processes to meet the time scale required.

'After an uneventful take-off we climbed steadily through light overcast to cruising height. We were probably more relaxed than usual because "Fitz" Fitzsimmons, our engineer, gave us more verses than ever of his favourite tune, "McNamara's Band".

'I recall our placid cruise over France towards Switzerland. "Dizzy" had informed us that we were southeast of Paris and a little east of track but that he would adjust the next leg of our course. I was listening to a Home Service broadcast to get the latest news bulletin and "Lofty" Maddocks, bomb aimer/front gunner, was having a leak into a suitable container.

'Our reverie was suddenly broken and I recall the events that followed as:

'Gunner: "There is a twin engined aircraft astern to port."

'Pilot: "Keep ... "

'He was interrupted by a rattle of hits on the aircraft. I remember that I drew my legs up to screen more of myself behind the armour plating to my rear. "Dizzy" Spillers raced past me on his way to his astrodome position.

'A gunner's voice said: "Christ ... "

'A glow appeared in my window.

'Pilot: "Prepare to abandon aircraft — I can't control — Abandon — Abandon."

'I took off my helmet — opened the floor hatch — detached the hatch cover and thrust it through the opening — clipped on my parachute and dived out of the hatch opening into the gloom. I do not remember pulling the ripcord but recall being almost immediately tightly squeezed by the harness when the 'chute opened and checked my drop and the silence and solitude that ensued as I drifted down in the light of the rising moon. Occasionally quite fierce swings developed as I passed through some light cloud and I was relieved to find that I could correct these by pulling on one or other of the shroud lines.

'I do not recall hearing or seeing anything of the aircraft at this time.

'It seems to take a long time to reach the ground — perhaps ten minutes — and then there was enough moonlight to illuminate

come cables below me. I heaved on a shroud and slid to one side of these — collapsing on the ground in what I thought might be the approved manner. I was disconsolate to find that I had left my cigarettes behind in the aircraft.

'I gathered up my parachute and harness and looked around for somewhere to hide them. After walking along a nearby road I came to a cemetery and finding a newly occupied grave buried the 'chute and harness in the conveniently soft earth. I walked back to the cemetery gates,

Below *'Lofty' Maddocks's recollection of the action, taken from a series of sketches done by him in the POW camp in Germany. The book that contained them was lost on the long march home, and subsequently picked up by a Canadian POW who took it to Canada. It had been returned to Maddocks by the Canadian government just prior to my contacting him in 1982.*

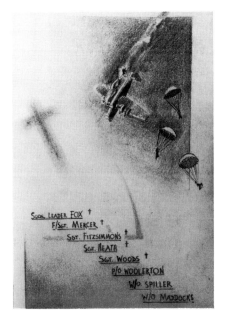

Sqdn. Leader FOX †
F/Sgt. Mercer †
Sgt. Fitzsimmons †
Sgt. Heath
Sgt. Woods †
P/o Woolerton
W/o Spiller
W/o Maddocks

sat on my folded Sidcot suit, leaned back against the gate pillar and took a grateful long drag at the half cigarette I had found in my pocket. It was the one I had put out before boarding at Elsham Wolds.

'Opening my escape kit tin, I took out a compass to identify a south-westerly direction and set off walking to get away from the scene. I walked across country, avoiding main roads or habitation. After walking till dawn I rested a while then kept going but keeping to cover and avoiding roads. Towards dusk I looked down on a biggish village with a church suitably placed to approach in the dark. I knocked at the door of the church house and asked for the priest.

'I was led to an office and after a little while a priest came. I identified myself as an English airman and made known my need for a pair of shoes or boots to replace my flying boots which by then were giving me hell. The priest appeared to be helpful — he absented himself for a while then reappeared and led me through the village to a house which we entered. There were about a dozen villagers there in a largish room and within minutes a gendarme appeared with a drawn revolver and a similarly armed gendarme appeared at a door on the other side of the room. I was escorted by these two to the local police station. About an hour later German soldiers appeared and I was taken to Bar-le-Duc, given coffee and bread at a street cafe, where, after a two or three hour wait, two German air force officers took me in charge and drove me to St Dizier in a Volkswagen Beetle. After the remainder of the night in a cell on the station I was escorted to the Adjutant's office where I sat for some time before being introduced to a young pilot who claimed to have shot us down.

'He spoke good English — said he had spent some time in England — did not attempt to "pump" me at all for Service information — said he was surprised there had been so little reaction from us before he attacked and that he regretted that all our crew had not survived. He gave me a couple of cigarettes and left.

'Later that day I was taken, under escort, by bus, train and tram to Dulag Luft near Frankfurt to await a significant gathering of RAF survivors to make up a party for transport to Stalag Luft III at Sagan. At the time of being shot down my rank was Pilot Officer signals leader and my number 49754.'

Having read the story as it unfolded through the reasearches, through their tortuous twists and turns, I hope you will feel as one American did who wrote to me after reading *Combat Medals of the Third Reich*. 'You will indeed receive numerous letters of congratulations, not least from self acclaimed experts such as myself. My qualifications differ, however, in that my introduction to this entire subject was from the martial rather than the materialistic standpoint. I am also amongst those who initially did not view the Swastika, Hakenkreuz as I knew it, with unqualified hatred. Be that as it may, I know the subject better than most and forty years on, with the benefit of both personal experience and hindsight, I am able to humbly assure you that you have recaptured the

Above *Wollerton (on the left) describes room 4 in the Stalag Luft III POW camp: 'The room, or "Kriegie", was about 14' square, and was home for eight of us at this time; two Americans and a New Zealand chap are missing from the snap. The stove, made from Canadian powdered milk containers, was all our own work, designed by Frank Knight, the chap on the left of it, who was a wizard with tin, and even made a weight-driven pendulum clock from tin. Knight was the sole survivor of a Hudson which had hit the mast of a merchant ship in the Skaggerak, which it had been attempting to bomb by shaking the bombs from the racks, the release mechanism having frozen. Frank, who was in the turret, came to his senses still in it, perched on an ice flow with no sign of the rest of the aircraft. He stepped out of it into the dinghy floating nearby, just as it slid off the flow and under the waves. Having taken the basket of pigeons with him from the turret, he placed them behind him in the dinghy whilst he wrote a message. Unfortunately, unnoticed by him, the pigeons drowned in a foot of water. The attacked merchant ship, which picked him up, had a Swedish captain who was sympathetic, and gave Frank his address. This resulted in correspondence between Frank and the captain's daughter, who very kindly sent lots of parcels, some of which he got.'*

spirit of the subject as, for better or worse, it actually existed and that is all that counts.' He went on to say, 'I wish that it had been available years ago when the spirit of my youth burned even more brightly. Now that I am well into senior citizenship (how cozily Americans express things) I find it a splendid and welcome reminder of those days.' Albeit this is a very floral tribute, I feel that it epitomizes my own feelings of historical endeavour.

To the question, 'What to collect?', I can only say, go for quality; it is far better to have six exceptional items, in terms of quality, than a room full of junk. Research the material fully before parting with the hard-earned cash and follow the gut feelings. If it feels original and good, it usually is. If, however, you have doubts at the beginning, they usually grow and a collection founded on such pieces will give no long-term pleasure.

From the medals and awards

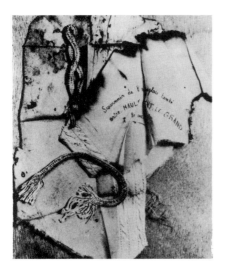

Above *A piece of parachute taken by a French official from the crash site of 'D for Donald' and retained as a souvenir. Albert Flipts has been in contact with the local priest who informed him that there are still pieces of the plane at the site. It is hoped to recover a piece to complete the story.*

Below *The Scroll of Honour given to the next of kin. A sad reminder of bravery.*

GVI   RI

This scroll commemorates
Squadron Leader S. H. Fox, D.F.M.
Royal Air Force
held in honour as one who
served King and Country in
the world war of 1939-1945
and gave his life to save
mankind from tyranny. May
his sacrifice help to bring
the peace and freedom for
which he died.

included in this book and those in *Combat Medals of the Third Reich*, it is hoped that you will discover one or more of the themes that can be employed when embarking on collecting. Collecting on a theme basis (such as the badges of naval, air force or army units) is something which is winning much popularity. Collectors now, especially the more advanced, are tending to collect flying awards and insignia of either one country, one continent or one particular war. This is true for both the other Services, of course.

Another theme that is worthy of note, is that of the battle of Arnhem. This gives the medal collector, wargamer, military modeller or militaria collector scope to collect the awards of Great Britain, America, Poland, Czechoslovakia, the underground organizations of Holland as well as those of the German forces including the Waffen-SS, Labour Corps and certain Foreign Volunteer units in a microcosm of the whole war encompassing a time scale of just approximately fourteen days. This has the advantages of limiting what one should collect, but allowing the collector the freedom of collecting medals, badges and insignia as well as the uniforms and other pieces of equipment that were used in the time scale. One particular fault among many collectors is their inability to keep to defined collecting guidelines, giving a jackdaw-like appearance to their collections. My advice to the more advanced collector is to stick to the guidelines you have established and try to make as complete as possible the series that you have embarked upon.

Index to British Orders, Medals, Decorations and Awards common to all Services and awarded to Britain's allies

GB.D001 The Victoria Cross — 29 January 1856

This decoration is possibly the most renowned of any in the world, its simplicity belying the unequivocal acts of bravery required to receive a bestowal of this award. From its inception on 29 January 1856, it has become progressively more difficult to win, to such an extent that up until 1987 only 1,354 Crosses and three first Bars have been awarded. The last two Crosses were posthumous awards for the attack on Goose Green by the Paras in the Falklands' conflict. In fact the Cross is becoming almost always a posthumous award.

The history and general evolution of the Cross cannot be covered in this work but I strongly recommend the reader to further study of the subject. This book, being about Second World War decorations, allows only for a thumbnail sketch of the history of this Herculean badge of self-sacrifice. Queen Victoria's Prince Consort Albert first suggested the award to reward the bravery of troops in the Crimea for which no other distinction existed. The design of the Cross is attributed to H.H. Armstead, although some reference has been made by Hancock & Co to indicate that Prince Albert had a great hand in its development, and it has been produced by this company throughout the period of its existence. It is usually made from the barrels of Russian guns captured in the Crimean War. However, during the First World War it is reliably suggested that the Cross was produced from Chinese cannon. It is also believed that the bronze from the Russian guns used for the original production of the crosses was exhausted in 1942.

The first awards were announced in the *London Gazette* of 24 February 1857. There were 111 recipients for the Crimean War and Queen Victoria held a great investiture in Hyde Park on 26 June 1857 at which she personally invested 62 of the recipients with great ceremony.

The design of the Cross has not changed during its life but the ribbon has: initially awards to the Navy had a dark blue ribbon and those of the Army a crimson one. However, with the introduction of the RAF as a formal third arm of Britain's military forces on 1 April 1918, and the re-evaluation of awards for this new Service, it was decided that the Victoria Cross should be the highest award to be rendered to all three Services and thus, that the ribbon should be the same for each Service. It was deemed appropriate that the crimson ribbon should be the one universally adopted and this has been the case ever since.

The obverse design comprises a bronze, straight-armed cross pattée with raised edge. This is followed by a similar inner edge line inset by 2 mm. The field produced between the two lines is pebbled. The centre of the cross has a central medallion which has a single matching line. Into the field of this medallion is positioned, at the bottom, a Victorian crown surmounted by a lion standing on all fours, head facing full face towards the viewer. The upper part and tail are placed on the upper arm of the cross.

The lion has a crown on its head, while a scroll covers the line of the medallion at the centre, with a raised edge line at top and bottom. This scroll folds over and then back over each of the horizontal arms of the cross, with V cuts into each end of the scroll. The points are finished with pellets. The field of the scroll is pebbled and on to it is placed the inscription, in small raised capitals, 'FOR VALOUR'. This inscription runs from the lower edge of the horizontal arm of the cross on the left (as viewed from the front) to the relevant position on the arm of the cross on the right. The legend is garnished at the beginning and end by a bouquet of flowers. The upper arm has a solid semi-circular projection, with a hole through it to allow for a suspension ring which passes through it and into a capital V, which forms the lower part of the suspension bar. This comprises a bow directly above the V, with laurel leaves running in opposite directions from either side, these being thus diametrically opposed. Above this is a cut-out portion to allow the ribbon to pass through.

The reverse design follows that of the obverse, save that the crown and lion are omitted. Thus the medallion is exposed and, in this case, it has an inner matching line to that of the inner line of the arms of the cross.

The Cross was issued named, and in the case of those awarded during the Second World War, name, rank, serial number and unit are engraved in plain capitals on the reverse of the bar, while the date of the award is engraved in three lines on the central medallion. For subsequent awards, a

Bar similar to that of the suspension bar was added as a slip-on. This had the date of the award engraved on the reverse. There were 182 awards of the Cross and one first Bar during the Second World War.

The Cross can be conferred upon officers, non-commissioned officers and men of all three armed forces as well as members of the merchant marine and auxiliary forces under military command. Women are also eligible for the award, although none have so far received one. Civilians can also be awarded the Cross if they are caught up in fighting and come under the control of the armed forces. The original warrant was extended by a warrant of 22 May 1920, with the words of qualification, 'Most con-spicuous bravery or some daring or pre-eminent act of valour or self sacrifice or extreme devotion to duty in the presence of the enemy'. I consider every award of the Victoria Cross to be a story in its own right and this book can only open the doors to further reading on the subject, as the history of these exploits has already filled many volumes and this short description can do nothing to demonstrate the heroism and self sacrifice shown by the recipients of the Cross.

The ribbon measures 38 mm and is of crimson red; when worn on the undress uniform, a miniature of the Cross is worn. To indicate that a Bar has been bestowed a second miniature is applied.

GB.D002 The George Cross — 24 September 1940

The Cross was instituted on 24 September 1940 by George VI in recognition of the need to reward the valour of those civilians and military personnel who were subject to attack by the enemy behind the lines in what, up until then, would have been considered safe territory, either the homeland or provinces under control of the British government. This situation had been brought about by the advances of mechanized warfare and the indiscriminate bombing of Great Britain. Such instances of the award of the Cross include, for example, the moving of a burning ammunition train which was set to explode, the fire having been started by faulty brakes. This action by a railwayman from March, in Cambridgeshire, saved a town.

The Cross was awarded to the island of Malta in April 1942 to reward the people as a whole for the deprivations and the bombing that they suffered at the hands of the Germans and Italians in the cause of the British war effort. The Cross was designed to replace the Empire Gallantry Medal, which is outside the scope of this work, but I will mention it for the sake of completeness. In 1971 surviving holders of the Albert Medal and Edward Medals were also enabled to exchange their medals for the George Cross, so the original idea of this Cross being the non-combatants' version of the Victoria Cross has been fully implemented.

The obverse design comprises a straight armed cross, with a raised field inset by aproximately 1 mm. At the centre is a medallion with a raised edge line, with a further raised field inset by approximately 2 mm. The field produced has the inscription, in raised capitals running from the bottom of the horizontal left arm to the bottom of the corresponding right arm, 'FOR GALLANTRY'. This inscription is preceded and finished by a pellet and between these pellets there is a small ornate emblem.

The quarters have the stylized monogram, GVI, while the raised medallion has St George and the Dragon. This higher relief was introduced from about 1944. From the upper arm of the cross is a small lug with a hole through which is placed a small ring, that goes through a similar one on the base of the ribbon suspender bar. This suspender is sim-ilar to the one found on the Victoria Cross (GB.D001) and is a flat bar. In this case it has a 1 mm raised end that runs upwards and is repeated across the top to form a slit to allow the ribbon to be passed through it and the bar. The field of the bar is adorned with laurel leaves which point in opposite directions, ten in each branch. The Cross is produced in silver. The reverse is plain, save for the naming of the recipient (which includes rank and service, if applicable) and the date of the award. There is provision for a Bar but none have been awarded so far.

The Cross can be awarded to any person, male or female, who has rendered acts of conspicuous gallantry when not in the face of the enemy. It can also be awarded posthumously.

The ribbon is blue and 38 mm wide and when worn alone, as on a Service tunic, carries a small miniature emblem of the Cross.

GB.D003 The George Medal — 24 September 1940

This Medal was introduced on 24 September 1940 at the same time as the George Cross (GB.D002) and was intended to reward people for similar but lesser acts of bravery.

The obverse design consists of the crowned effigy of George VI with, at the truncation of the head, in small raised capitals, the initials of the designer, PM, representing Percy Metcalfe. The medal has a raised edge rim and the circumscription 'GEOR-GIVS VI D: G: BR: OM N: REX ET INDIAE IMP:'.

The reverse design comprises a raised edge with, on the field, George and the Dragon. The dragon is on its hind legs, wings semi-outstretched with St George's lance through its body, point protruding from its chest. The inscription 'THE GEORGE MEDAL' is placed round the edge, with 'THE' placed between the ground and the tail of the horse

Above *Obverse The Victoria Cross (GB.D001)*

Above right *Obverse The George Cross (GB.D002)* (Spink & Son Ltd)

Right *Reverse The George Medal (GB.D003)* (Spink & Son Ltd)

Above left *Reverse The Distinguished Service Order (GB.D004)* (Spink & Son Ltd)

Above *Reverse Order of the British Empire Gallantry George VI type (GB.D005)* (Spink & Son Ltd)

Left *Reverse The Distinguished Service Cross George VI type (GB.D006). An example of a privately engraved name.* (Spink & Son Ltd)

Above *Reverse The Distinguished Service Medal George VI First type (GB.D007)* (Spink & Son Ltd)

Above right *Obverse Military Cross George VI First type (GB.D009)* (Spink & Son Ltd)

Right *Reverse Military Medal George VI First type (GB.D010)*

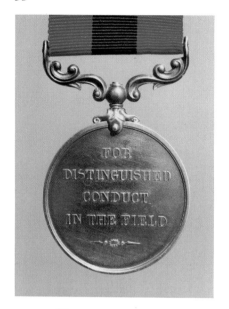

Above left *Reverse The Distinguished Conduct Medal (GB.D011)* (Spink & Son Ltd)

Above *Reverse The Distinguished Flying Cross George VI First type (GB.D012)* (Spink & Son Ltd)

Left *Reverse The Conspicuous Gallantry Medal [Flying] (GB.D014)* (Spink & Son Ltd)

and 'GEORGE' between the tail and St George's elbow, while 'MEDAL' is placed between the bottom of the horse's mouth and the tip of the left wing of the dragon. The reverse design was taken from a book plate designed for the royal library at Windsor by Stephen Gooden; this was adapted to that used on the reverse of the medal by George Kruger Gray.

From the top of the Medal is a small ramp with a ball surmounting it, through which is placed the ribbon ring suspender.

The Medal is issued named and this is found on its rim. There are differences in the style of naming during the period of the award which also reflect a civilian or military recipient. For subsequent awards a Bar of the slip-on variety was authorized; it is a flat bar with, superimposed upon it at the centre, a small bow with, from either side, six laurel leaves that are staggered with seven laurel berries placed in their angles. The reverse of the Bar has the year of the award engraved upon it. There were 1,387 Medals and twenty first Bars awarded during the period of the Second World War.

The ribbon of the medal is 32 mm wide and pink red in colour, with five blue stripes measuring 2 mm and spaced 4 mm apart.

GB.D004 The Distinguished Service Order — 9 November 1886

The Order was introduced on 9 November 1886 to reward officers of all Services for gallantry or distinguished service, including from 1943 officers in the Merchant Navy operating under Royal Naval command. The normal practice up until this time had been to reward such services through promotion but this had led to anomalies in various situations and it was thus decided to confer a cross instead. It can only be awarded to someone who has previously been Mentioned in Despatches, and ranks only slightly lower then the Victoria Cross. The history and general evolution of the order is outside the scope of the book but it should be noted that there are variations in the design of the obverse throughout its history and that, while the original crosses were produced in gold, later ones are in silver gilt. It is a particularly elegant award and makes a good series to collect, the various types ranging over 100 years.

The obverse of the George VI type that was used during the Second World War, comprises a cross with arms that slope upwards, with convex ends. Thus the quadrants formed are

Below *Obverse The Distinguished Service Order (GB.D004)* (Spink & Son Ltd)

of a semi-circular design. The outer edges of the arms of the cross have an outline and the field produced is filled with opaque white enamel. The centre of the cross has a wreath of laurel leaves with a bow at the base. The laurel leaves are enamelled green, there being fourteen in each side in pairs, each bunch separated from that below by a laurel berry which is picked out in red enamel. The central field of the wreath is finished in red translucent enamel, with straight lines showing from beneath it giving a sunray effect. On this field is the royal crown.

The reverse is the same as the obverse, with the exception of the crown which is replaced by the monogram of George VI, which is surmounted by a king's crown. The cross is formed hollow, from two parts and constructed in silver, with all the exposed metal parts being gilded.

From the upper arm of the cross is a circular eyelet, through which is placed a ring that attaches it to the suspension bar. This bar is an oblong box with a raised edge line, and on the recessed field are placed two sprigs of laurel leaves, tied at the centre with a bow and diametrically opposed. From the top of the ribbon is an identical bar with, on the reverse, a pin and hook for attachment to the uniform.

For subsequent awards of the Order a Bar was authorized which comprises an oblong box with a raised spine, on to which, at the centre, is applied a crown, the orb of which breaks the upper line of the bar. The Order is issued unnamed but the bar is engraved on the reverse with the date of the award. 4,880 crosses, 497 first Bars, 59 second Bars and eight third Bars were awarded during the period of the Second World War.

The ribbon is 29 mm wide, of purple-red with dark blue edge stripes 6 mm wide. When only the ribbon is worn on the Service tunic a silver rosette is pinned to the ribbon to denote a Bar.

GB.D005 Order of the British Empire — Gallantry — 29 December 1922

This medal was originally introduced on 24 August 1917 and was of a totally different design to the later version introduced on 29 December 1922. This medal was discontinued with the introduction of the George Cross (GB.D002) on 24 September 1940 and earlier recipients had to exchange it for the newly instituted Cross. Four posthumous awards were rendered during the period of the Second World War, which were exchanged, and one honorary award made to a French national. This is the sole award that could be worn after the institution of the George Cross, as foreign nationals are not eligible for the award of the latter decoration. I have not included a description of the medal or ribbon because it is not, properly speaking, a Second World War decoration.

Awards to the Royal Navy

This book cannot possibly discuss the contribution of the Royal Navy during the Second World War, but thought about some of its areas of operations should give some ideas for thematic collections. The Atlantic, Arctic and Malta convoys, the 'big ship' actions involving battleships and carriers and their miniature counterparts including submarines, Motor Torpedo Boats or even canoes are all subjects worthy of attention. The attack on the French Fleet, the Dieppe raid, the north African, Sicilian, Italian and Normandy landings, which would all have been impossible without the Royal Navy, are all subjects equally worthy of consideration when thinking about a theme. The flying badges and awards to the Fleet Air Arm in its various actions are especially attractive to many collectors. (Indian and Pacific Ocean operations are equally valid but outside the scope of this volume.)

Index to Royal Naval Awards

Flying insignia

GB.D006 The Distinguished Service Cross — 15 June 1901

This Cross was initially known as the Conspicuous Service Cross when it was introduced on 15 June 1901. The name and conditions for the award of the decoration were changed on 14 October 1914 and these have remained in force, basically unchanged except for fine tuning, until the present time. However, the scope of this book only takes in the George VI first type, which comprises a silver cross with chamfered edges. The arms of the cross give the quarters a semi-circular design and have a plain flat field. At the centre of the cross is a raised circle with the monogram of George VI in plain capitals, surmounted by a stylized crown. From the top arm is an eyelet, through which passes the ribbon ring. The reverse is plain and since 1940 the date of the award has been engraved on the lower arm. The medal was issued unnamed but it is

sometimes encountered with the name unofficially applied by the recipient or, in the case of posthumous awards by the relatives.

On 17 September 1916 a Bar was authorized. It is silver with a 'slip on' method of attachment and the design has remained the same throughout the period of its existence. It has a plain, slightly convex obverse with raised ends, top and bottom, at each end of the bar. The centre has a raised imperial crown applied to it, with the orb breaking the upper line of the bar. As with the Cross, since 1940 the date of the award has been engraved on the reverse of the Bar. 4,524 Crosses, 434 first Bars, 44 second Bars and one third Bar were awarded during the period of the Second World War.

The Cross was to reward naval and Royal Marine officers with the rank of Commander and below who had performed acts of distinguished service which did not permit the award of the Distinguished Service Order (GB.D004). This was extended on 20 December 1939 to officers of the fleet of the rank or equivalent rank of Commander and Lieutenant Commander and foreign naval officers of corresponding rank. Officers and warrant officers of the RAF serving with the fleet were made eligible for the award on 17 April 1940. Army officers and warrant officers serving in defensively equipped merchant ships became eligible on 5 November 1942. RAF officers and warrant officers serving afloat, but not with the fleet, became eligible on 13 January 1943. It could be awarded to officers of the WRNS for gallantry and distinguished conduct on shore during enemy action and to merchant navy officers working with the Royal Navy.

The ribbon measures 32 mm and comprises a dark blue band with a 12 mm central white stripe. To denote the award of a Bar when only the ribbon is worn, a silver rosette is added to the central white stripe.

Above *Obverse The Distinguished Service Cross George VI type (GB.D006)* (Spink & Son Ltd)

GB.D007 The Distinguished Service Medal — 14 October 1914

During the Second World War this Medal comprised an obverse design that depicts the crowned effigy of George VI with, at the truncation of the head in small raised capital letters, 'PM' for the designer Percy Metcalfe. It has the circumscription, 'GEORGIVS VI D: G: BR: OMN: REX ET INDIAE IMP:'. The reverse design comprises a raised edge line and a flat field on to which is placed a wreath of laurel leaves, with an interlaced double bow tie at the base. Between the arms at the apex a Victorian crown surmounts the inscription, in three lines, 'FOR, DISTINGUISHED, SERVICE'. From 27 June 1916 a Bar was authorized for those who performed subsequent acts of service before the enemy. This takes the form of an oblong box, with raised edge line, while on the recessed field are placed two rows of laurel leaves pointing horizontally in opposing directions, with a bow at the centre. This is the same type of Bar that is used on the Military Medal (GB.D010), the Distinguished Conduct Medal (GB.D011) and the Conspicuous Gallantry Medal (RN) (GB.D008).

The Medal was issued named with the man's name, rank, serial number and, in some cases, the ship on which he was serving. There are varying forms of naming encountered from the inception of the medal and in some cases, the type of action is also included on the medal rim. The Bar for awards during the 1939-45 period is undated. There were 7,132 Medals, 153 first Bars, four second Bars and one third Bar awarded during the period of the Second World War.

The ribbon suspension bar is of the ball and claw fitting, with straight plain arms. The early examples of the suspender swivel but in 1941 a fixed type was introduced, although onhand stocks, it seems very likely, were still issued until the following year or until they were exhausted.

The Medal was to reward naval and Royal Marines personnel with the rank of Petty Officer or below, who had performed acts of distinguished service. This was extended on 20 December 1939 to Petty Officers and below of the fleet and foreign naval personnel of corresponding rank. NCOs and men of the RAF serving with the fleet were made eligible for the award on 17 April 1940. Army NCOs and below, serving in defen-

Above *Obverse The Distinguished Service Medal George VI First type (GB.D007)* (Spink & Son Ltd)

sively equipped merchant ships, became eligible on 5 November 1942. RAF NCOs and men serving afloat but not with the fleet, became eligible on 13 January 1943. It could be awarded to the equivalent ranks of women in the WRNS for gallantry and distinguished conduct on shore during enemy action. Merchant marine personnel of equivalent rank, who were working with the Royal Navy, were also eligible for the award under the same circumstances and conditions.

The ribbon measures 32 mm wide and is of navy blue, with central white stripes 5 mm wide set 1 mm apart. To denote the award of a Bar when only the ribbon is worn, a silver rosette is added to the ribbon.

GB.D008 The Conspicuous Gallantry Medal (RN) — 13 August 1855

The history of this medal dates back to the Crimean War and I can only give the briefest of outlines. It was reviewed in 1874 at the end of the Ashanti War and was reinstituted on 7 July 1874 as the Conspicuous Gallantry Medal. It continued with various small modifications up to the Second World War with a final reorganization on 15 January 1943, when part of the medal was separated to produce the Conspicuous Gallantry Medal (Flying) (GB.D014).

The obverse design comprises the crowned effigy of George VI with, at the truncation of the head, in small raised capitals, 'PM', the initials of the designer Percy Metcalfe. The edge has a raised rim and the circumscription, 'GEORGIVS VI D: G: BR: OM N: REX ET INDIAE IMP:'. The reverse design comprises a raised edge rim, which produces a flat field, on which is a wreath of laurel leaves, with an interlaced double bow tie at the base. Between the arms of the wreath, at the apex, is a Victorian crown surmounting, in three lines, the inscription, 'FOR, CONSPICUOUS, GALLANTRY', beneath which is a pellet, flanked on either side by a stylized spearhead.

It is suspended from the top by a ball and claw straight bar of the swivel type. The Medal was issued named and numerous types are encountered during its history. A Bar was authorized in 1916 but only one has ever been awarded. It takes the form of an oblong box, with raised edge. On the field thus produced is a spray of laurel leaves pointing horizontally in opposing directions, on either side of a bow. This type of Bar was used on the Military Medal (GB.D010) and the Distinguished Conduct Medal (GB.D011). The date of the award is not added to the Bar. During the Second World War eighty medals were awarded but no Bars.

This Medal is the rarest of all the gallantry medals, being only awarded 243 times from its inception up until 1946. It was to reward Petty Officers and men of the Royal Navy and non-commissioned officers and men of the Royal Marines who distinguished themselves by acts of conspicuous

Above *Reverse The Conspicuous Gallantry Medal [RN] (GB.D008)* (Spink & Son Ltd)

gallantry in action with the enemy. NCOs and men of the RAF serving with the fleet were made eligible for the award on 17 April 1940. NCOs and men of the Army, serving in defensively equipped merchant ships, became eligible on 1 July 1942. Merchant marine personnel of a status equivalent to that of Petty Officers or seamen in the Royal Navy, became eligible on 17 September 1942. RAF NCOs and men, serving afloat but not with the fleet, became eligible on 13 January 1943. It could also be awarded to equivalent ranks of the WRNS for gallantry and distinguished conduct on shore during enemy action. The ribbon comprises a 32 mm white band, with edge stripes of blue 5 mm wide.

Flying insignia of the Navy
GB.N001 Royal Navy Fleet Air Arm Pilots' Wings — 1937-1952

This badge comprises a pair of wings constructed of three lines of fletching. The top line was produced as one continuous line of embroidery, the stitches being formed in a diagonal pattern, running left to right. The downward sweep at the end of the wing, forming the outer edge, is executed in stitching that runs in the opposite direction and separated by a black cotton thread. The line below comprises seven short pin feathers, with the stitches executed diagonally from right to left and their outer edge picked out in black cotton. There is a larger feather at the end, with the embroidery stitching executed in the opposite direction to that of its counterpart feathers but matching that of the feathers that produce the lower line. This line has eight feathers, longer than the others but ending in line with the aforementioned individual feather. The other wing is identical to the one described but is in a mirror configuration. The centre of the wing is made up of an open work

Above *Royal Navy Fleet Air Arm Pilots' Wings (GB.N001)*

wreath, that is to say the laurel leaves are individual as opposed to being tightly wrapped with a bow at the base and a crown at the apex between the two arms of the wreath.

In the wreath's field is a fouled anchor. The anchor chain and outline of the crown are executed in silver bullion wire. The anchor is produced in silver metal, the wings are executed in gold wire, the crown's insets are of red velvet and the whole design is executed on a black melton backing. The badge measures 78 mm from wingtip to wingtip and 33 mm vertically.

The wings are worn over the left

breast pocket when worn on the white and khaki uniforms and on the

left cuff of the blue uniform above the rank loop insignia.

GB.N002 Royal Navy Fleet Air Arm Other Ratings Pilots' Wings [Red]
GB.N003 Royal Navy Fleet Air Arm Other Ratings Pilots' Wings [Blue]

This pair of wings is of identical design to that of the officers but executed in cotton thread of either red on a dark wool background, or blue on a white background. Both versions of this badge measure 81 mm wingtip to wingtip and 37 mm vertically. The difference between the two badges is that the red was to be used on the standard Service tunic or khaki uniform, while the blue was for wear on the summer uniform.

GB.N004 Royal Navy Fleet Air Arm Officer Observer or Acting Officer Observer — 1942-1952

These wings comprise a pair of upward pointing wings with a straight line of embroidery to represent the fletching that is executed in stitching that runs diagonally right to left, with a wingtip that slopes at approximately 45 degrees at the top. Beneath this is a row of pin feathers, five in number, but these are not individually picked out, only round the edges of the first and last and the tips of each of the individual feathers. The lower feathers that form the third row number nine and run from the top tip and round the second row, joining the central device which is an 'O'. The feathers in this row are individually picked out with black cotton thread. The opposite wing is a mirror image of the wing described. The 'O' is produced by diagonal

Above *Royal Navy Fleet Air Arm Officer Observer or Acting Officer Observer Wings (GB.N004)*

threads that run round it and these have an outer and inner line of wire. Surmounting the 'O' is a king's crown. The central field has a fouled anchor made of silver metal while the rope is of bullion. The design is executed in gold wire for the wings, silver wire for the 'O' and the anchor chain while the crown is in gold wire with red velvet insets. The badge was produced on a dark blue backing and measures 52 mm horizontally and 35 mm vertically. These wings were worn on the left cuff of the blue naval tunic.

GB.N005 Royal Navy Fleet Air Arm Rating Observer or Acting Rating Observer [Red]
GB.N006 Royal Navy Fleet Air Arm Rating Observer or Acting Rating Observer [Blue]

These two badges are of the same basic design as GB.N004 but are executed in red embroidery on to a dark blue background and blue on to a white background. The red version was worn on the blue naval uniform on the left cuff, while the blue version was for wear on the white summer uniform.

GB.N007 Royal Navy Fleet Air Arm Warrant Officer Air Gunner — 1942

These wings are identical to GB.N004 but with the 'O' substituted by a rope circle. The method of wear and the colours of the embroidery are also identical.

Right *Royal Navy Fleet Air Arm Warrant Officer Air Gunner Wings (GB.N007)*

GB.N008 Royal Navy Fleet Air Arm Rating Air Gunner [Red]
GB.N009 Royal Navy Fleet Air Arm Rating Air Gunner [Blue]

These two wings are identical to their counterparts GB.N005 and GB.N006. Again, as in the previous badge GB.N007, the 'O' has been replaced by a rope circle. The method of wear and the colour of the badges are also identical.

GB.N010 Royal Navy Fleet Air Arm Officers, Telegraphist Air Gunner [1st, 2nd, 3rd and Acting 3rd Class] — September 1942

These wings were introduced in September 1942 for acting air gunners who held warrant officer or higher rank. They are identical to GB.N007 but with the omission of the crown surmounting the rope wreath. The colours of the embroidery also match those of the previously described badge GB.N007.

Right *Royal Navy Fleet Air Arm Officers', Telegraphist Air Gunner [First, Second, Third and Acting Third Class] Wings (GB.N010)*

GB.N011 Royal Navy Fleet Air Arm Ratings, Telegraphist Air Gunner [1st, 2nd, 3rd and Acting 3rd Class] (Red)
GB.N012 Royal Navy Fleet Air Arm Ratings, Telegraphist Air Gunner [1st, 2nd 3rd and Acting 3rd Class] (Blue)

These wings were introduced in September 1942 for acting air gunners who held rank below warrant officer. They are identical to GB.N008 and GB.N009 but with the omission of the crown that surmounts the rope wreath. The colouring of the embroidery on the wings also follows that of GB.N008 and GB.N009. They were worn by other ratings 38.1 mm above the point of the left cuff of the jumper or the end of the sleeve of the service jacket.

Left *Royal Navy Fleet Air Arm Ratings', Telegraphist Air Gunner [First, Second, Third and Acting Third Class] (Red) Wings (GB.N011)*

GB.N013 Royal Marines Pilots' Wings

This brevet consisted of a pair of wings of the same design as those described in GB.N001 but the central wreath and crown was replaced by the flaming grenade. The flames are of an irregular design and beneath the grenade is a scroll with the inscription, 'UNIQUE'. The wings measure 85 mm wingtip to wingtip and 35 mm vertically. The grenade, letters and outline of the scroll are executed in gold wire. The wings are executed in silver wire while the scroll's field is produced in red silk embroidery. The whole of the design of the badge is produced on a red wool background. The wings are worn on the cuff above the rank stripes, on the lower left sleeve.

Above *Royal Marines Pilots' Wings (GB.N013)*

GB.N014 Royal Marines Observers' Wing — 1942

This wing comprises an 'O' with one wing attached, similar to that of the RAF with a crown surmounting the 'O'. The wing is of the same general design as that found on GB.N004 but at a more gentle angle. The wing is of gold wire embroidery, the 'O' is of silver, the crown is gold with red velvet insets and it is worked on to a blue background.

Awards to the British Army

The theatres of operations covered by this book are the European mainland, the Mediterranean and North Africa. In later sections on free forces units further mention will be made of specific campaigns, but bearing in mind the idea of creating a collection with a theme the same remarks apply as earlier for the Navy. (See also section on campaign medals and stars commencing on page 87). One concept which is gaining popularity is collecting the awards and other insignia, as well as complete uniforms, of the various elite units such as Popski's Private Army, the Long Range Desert Group or the Airborne divisions, and this is certainly something worth thinking about. Bear in mind, though, that in this as in all other fields of collecting, when a particular subject becomes popular prices inevitably rise, so you might be advised to seek out something less obvious which nevertheless appeals and which can form the basis of a logical collection.

Index to British Army Awards

Qualification Wings

GB.D009 Military Cross — 28 December 1914

This Cross was introduced on 28 December 1914 to reward officers for gallantry in the face of the enemy or under fire. The general design has remained the same from its institution, while only the royal cypher has changed with the various monarchs. The Cross was designed by E.C. Collins and takes the form of a cross with equal length arms. The arms are straight with a small outward curl at the ends. At the ends of each arm, with the orb just breaking the end line, is placed a king's crown which is raised above the flat field of the cross' arm. Superimposed on to the flat field is a further cross with a raised central spine on each of its arms. At its centre, superimposed, is the royal cypher of George VI, GRI. From the top of the upper arm is an eyelet through which runs a ring that attaches the cross to a similar eyelet on the ribbon bar suspender, which is a plain flat bar with a slit, approximately 2 mm wide, machined into it to allow the ribbon to pass through.

The reverse is plain and machined flat. In the Second World War the date of the award is engraved on to the lower arm of the cross. It was issued unnamed, but is sometimes encountered with the recipient's name and the action privately engraved on the reverse. For subsequent awards, a Bar was added to the ribbon, comprising a flat bar with a central spine running horizontally its full length. On the middle is placed a crown, similar to that found on the ends of the arm of the Cross. The date of the award of the bar is inscribed on the reverse of the Bar. During the Second World War, 10,386 Crosses, 482 first Bars and 24 second Bars were awarded.

The Medal, during the Second World War, could be awarded to warrant officers and above of the British Army, members of the Navy and air force of the equivalent rank for ground actions, as well as the forces of the allies fighting with the British under similar circumstances. The upper rank limit was Captain or war substantive Major.

The ribbon comprises a 32 mm band of three equal stripes of white, mauve and white. When the ribbon is worn on the undress uniform, a silver rosette is placed upon it to denote the award of a Bar.

GB.D010 Military Medal — 25 March 1916

The Medal was introduced to reward NCOs and below for bravery in the field, for which no other suitable medal was in existence. The design of the Medal utilized during the Second World War comprises an obverse design which depicts the crowned effigy of George VI with, at the

Above *Obverse Military Medal George VI First type (GB.D010)*

the centre and bunches of laurel leaves running in opposite directions from it. It was issued named with the rank, serial number and the unit to which the recipient belonged. There were 15,225 Medals, 164 first Bars and two second Bars awarded during the Second World War.

The Medal, during the Second World War, could be awarded to NCOs and below of the British Army, members of the Navy and air force of equivalent rank for ground actions, as well as the forces of the allies fighting with the British under similar circumstances.

The ribbon comprises a 32 mm band with 7 mm blue edge stripes, with five 4 mm stripes of white, red, white, red, white. When only the ribbon was worn, a silver rosette was applied to denote the award of a Bar.

truncation of the head, in small raised capital letters, 'PM' for the designer Percy Metcalfe. It has the circumscription 'GEORGIVS VI D: G: BR: OMN: REX ET INDIAE IMP:'. The reverse comprises a wreath of laurel leaves tied at the base with a pair of interlocking bows. The apex of the wreath is open with, positioned between the two arms, the Victorian crown. Beneath is the royal cypher of George VI and the inscription in four lines, 'FOR, BRAVERY, IN THE, FIELD'. The words 'Bravery' and 'Field' are larger than the others.

From the top of the Medal is a ball and claw suspender with scalloped edges. For subsequent awards a Bar was added to the ribbon, comprising a flat box bar with raised edge line. The field thus produced has a tie at

Below *Letter sent with an award of a decoration when it could not be personally conferred upon the recipient by the King.*

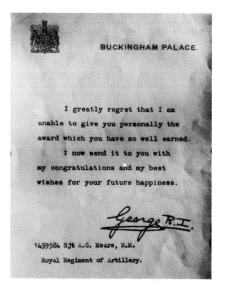

GB.D011 The Distinguished Conduct Medal

The design of this Medal comprises, for the Second World War, on the obverse, the crowned effigy of George VI with, beneath the truncation of the head, in small raised capitals, 'PM', the initials of the designer Percy Metcalfe. Round the edge is the circumscription, 'GEORGIVS VI D: G: BR: OMN: REX ET INDIAE IMP:'. The reverse has a raised edge line and a plain flat field, on to which is placed, in raised capitals in four lines, the inscription, 'FOR, DISTINGUISHED, CONDUCT, IN THE FIELD', with beneath, an elongated oval pellet flanked by a round pellet and a stylized arrowhead.

This Medal had a very involved evolution from its inception in the reign of Queen Victoria but this cannot be covered in this volume, only that which is relevant to the Second World War. The Medal was to reward NCOs of the Army for continuous devotion to duty. It was awarded named and with the recipient's rank, serial number and unit. For second or subsequent awards, a Bar of the laurel leaf type as employed in GB.D010 was awarded. This was of the slip-on type. In all during the Second World War 1,879 Medals and nineteen first Bars were awarded.

From the top of the medal is a suspender with a ball and claw fitting and scrolled arms. The ribbon is 32 mm wide and purple-red, with an 11 mm purple-blue centre stripe.

GB.a001 Army Air Corps Pilots' Wings — 1941-1952
GB.a001B Army Air Corps Pilot's Wings (Bullion)

These wings were introduced into the Army in 1941 and were employed to denote Army pilots. They comprise a pair of wings which have a short upper line of fletching, which is produced in continuous stitching. Beneath this is a line of individual feathers, these being short with, beneath them, a line of larger individual feathers, fourteen in number. These give a serrated edge to the lower line of the wing. The wings join at the roots on to a king's crown that forms the central design, which is surmounted by a lion who faces the viewer with the body pointing right to left. The wings measure 116 mm wingtip to wingtip and 43 mm from the base of the crown to the crown on the lion's head. The wings are executed in light blue silk, the lion in yellow silk, while its mouth is in red silk. The outline of the crown is yellow and white silk. The crown's liner is executed in red and yellow silk. The whole of the design is worked on to a dark blue melton backing.

The bullion version consists of silver wire embroidered wings. The crown and lion are in gold wire with red silk insets in the crown and lion's mouth. It has the same measurements as the cloth form and is worked on a dark blue wool background. The wings are worn on the left breast of the tunic, above the pocket or any medals or decorations.

Above *Army Air Corps Pilots' Wings* *(GB.a001)*

GB.a002 Army Air Corps Glider Pilots' Wings — 1942
GB.a002B Army Air Corps Glider Pilots' Wings (Bullion)

This badge comprises a pair of wings similar to GB.a001 but, in this case, they are smaller, measuring 72 mm wingtip to wingtip and 14 mm vertically. The centre of the wings has the crown and lion exchanged for an 'O', into which is placed a capital 'G' for Glider. The wings are executed in light blue silk, while the circle and the 'G' are produced in yellow. The bullion version is identical to the former badge with the wings in silver wire embroidery and the circle and 'G' in gold wire. It was issued to glider pilots on completion of training. The wings were worn on the left breast of the tunic, above the pocket or any medals or decorations.

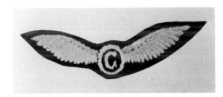

Above *Army Air Corps Glider Pilots' Wings* *(GB.a002)*

Awards to the Royal Air Force

It is impossible to cover in this chapter, let alone a whole series of books, the involvement of the RAF in the Second World War, its build-up from a peacetime run-down state, to the final days when it had reached the pinnacle of a supreme bombing and fighting force.

To reward the valour of the members of the embryo RAF, who up until 1 April 1918 had been receiving the relevant Army or naval awards, it was considered necessary to introduce a range of awards to replace but complement those of the Army and Navy. It was felt that these new awards would also signify the independence of the new Service from domination by either of the two older Services. A committee was set up to devise the format of the awards and in respect of gallantry awards, a range of four was suggested. These were to be the Distinguished Flying Cross (GB.D012) and the Air Force Cross (GB.D013) for officers, and the Distinguished Flying Medal (GB.D015) and the Air Force Medal (GB.D016) for other ranks. King George V gave his approval to the creation of these awards and decided that they should be 'brought out' on his birthday. To this effect, they were notified to the

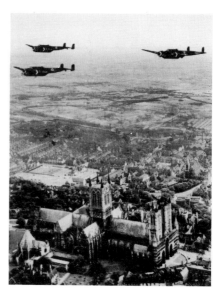

Above *Three Hampdens of Number 83 Squadron flying over Lincoln Cathedral* circa *February 1941. One, believed to be the lower left, is piloted by Squadron Leader [then Flight Sergeant] Sydney Fox.*

public in the *London Gazette* on 3 June 1918. However, it was not until 5 December 1919 that the warrant was published in the *Gazette*.

The wings of the various units are discussed as well as the medals that were awarded to the units of Fighter Command, Bomber Command,

Coastal Command, Transport Command and Special Forces, the Lysander Brigade which was so important to the covert activities in France and the Low Countries and helped the resistance groups in those countries. It was my decision to cover the flight insignia of these branches as they are again considered awards rather than simple qualification badges. From a collecting standpoint, they are often collected alongside those of the German air force and her Axis allies as a theme.

Index to Royal Air Force Awards

Insignia of the various Commands of the RAF

GB.D012 The Distinguished Flying Cross — 3 June 1918

The Cross had, from its original inception, retained the same obverse design that had been created by the Liverpool sculptor E. Carter Preston. This design comprises a cross that has a central boss with a laurel wreath formed of leaves tightly pushed together. The wreath has an inner raised line and the central field contains the monogram of the RAF encompassed by an endless cord in a fanciful design. Superimposed above the monogram and across the raised line and wreath, is the royal crown. At the wreath's base is positioned an ornate band that forms a tie which has an elegant tassle that drops on to the lower arm of the cross. The arms of the cross have curls at the ends that curl outwards, thus forming 'V's which are filled with flaming grenades on the horizontal and bottom arms, while the upper arm has a straight flame from the grenade that rises and leaves the top of the arm, whereupon it curls over producing an eyelet through which a ring is placed, allowing the cross to be attached to the suspender. From the central boss, from the raised inner line of the wreath, emanate a pair of wings that form the arm of the cross. The upper part or top line of the wing on either side, dictates the line of the arm of the cross. From the joint are two lines of fletching, with seven lines of individual feathers running from them. The vertical arms have the blades of a propeller superimposed upon them.

The suspender is a straight silver bar, ornamented with sprigs of laurel, and is connected to the cross by the silver ring. The reverse of the suspender is flat.

The reverse of the Cross is plain and polished with, at the centre, a round medallion which, in the case of those awarded during the Second World War, comprised an outer line with a raised and rounded centre and a similar inner line matching that found on the outside. On to the field is, in the upper part, the royal cypher of George VI and beneath, the date of the award's institution, 1918. The Cross is issued unnamed, but some recipients or their families, had them so inscribed particularly in the case of posthumous awards or in the case of recipients being killed in action afterwards. The date of the award is found engraved on the lower arm of the cross.

For subsequent awards, a Bar was added to the ribbon. This comprised a flat bar with a central spine running the full length horizontally. On the middle of the bar is a flying RAF eagle, looking to the right. The

Above *Obverse The Distinguished Flying Cross George VI First type (GB.D012)* (Spink & Son Ltd)

reverse of the Bar is flat and at either end at 90 degrees is a return that forms a box; these returns have a semicircular top and bottom, through which is placed a small hole. This type of bar is known as the slip-on type and, as its name suggests, was simply slipped over the ribbon of the medal. On the flat reverse, the date of the award is inscribed. During the Second World War, 1939-1945, 20,354 Crosses, 1,550 first Bars and 42 second Bars were awarded.

The Cross was to reward officers and warrant officers of the Royal Air Force and could subsequently be conferred on the equivalent ranks of the Army and Navy who were undertaking air activities with the RAF, as well as to foreign nationals flying with, or in conjunction with, the Royal Air Force for an act of valour, courage or devotion to duty occasioned whilst flying in active operations against the enemy. It was considered that the completion of forty operations against the enemy in bombing operations counted for the award of the Cross as a recognition for devotion to duty.

The ribbon comprises a 32 mm band with diagonal stripes of violet and white, running at an angle of 45 degrees from left to right. When only the ribbon is worn, a silver rosette is applied to denote the award of a Bar.

GB.D013 The Air Force Cross — 3 June 1918

The Cross has, from its original inception, retained the same obverse design, except that the cypher changed with the monarch and the post-war cuts in the territories that formerly comprised the British Empire. The Second World War version consists of a central boss or medallion, with a raised edge slightly inset with a round pellet at 12, 3, 6 and 9 o'clock respectively. This has an inner line. The field thus produced is slightly concave and has the figure of Hermes standing on a hawk's back, flying to the left. The design, as with the previous cross (GB.D012), was produced by the Liverpool sculptor, E. Carter Preston. From the boss are four arms that widen to the end, which have arrow points to represent thunderbolts. The upper arm has the royal crown superimposed. On to each arm is superimposed the rounded blade of a propeller with, from the rounded ends, an inverted V with, from its tip, a raised spine that runs to the boss. This spine, approximately 4 mm from the boss, broadens to a finger which then continues to the central medallion. The central medallion and fingers

Above *Obverse The Air Force Cross George VI First type with Bar*

thus produced are referred to as representing a bomb. In the angle of the V, starting from the top and running clockwise in capital letters are, G, I, VI, R. The angles of the cross are filled with three rows of fletching comprised of single distinct feathers. The design of the two lower quadrants is mirrored in the upper.

From the upper arm is an extension of the cross which is bent over to form a hook, to which is attached the suspender. One point of interest to note is that this hook sometimes becomes brittle and can break, thus losing the suspender which is nearly impossible for the collector to replace. The suspender is identical to the one found on the Distinguished Flying Cross (GB.D012) and comprises a straight silver bar ornamented with sprigs of laurel.

The reverse is plain, save for the centre which has a medallion identical to that found on the Distinguished Flying Cross with the cypher of George VI above the date 1918. During the war, the date of the award was engraved on the lower arm. The Cross was issued unnamed, although some recipients or their families had them suitably inscribed, particularly in the case of posthumous awards or upon the subsequent death of the recipient.

For subsequent awards, a slip-on Bar was added to the ribbon, comprising a flat bar with a central spine running the full length horizontally. On the middle is a flying Air Force eagle, looking to the right. The reverse of the bar is flat and at either end at 90 degrees is a return that forms a box. These returns have a semicircular top and bottom, through which a small hole is made. The date of the award of the Bar is inscribed on its flat reverse. During the Second World War 2,001 Crosses, 26 first Bars and one second Bar were awarded.

The Cross was to reward officers and warrant officers of the Royal Air Force and could subsequently be conferred on the equivalent ranks of the Army and Navy who were undertaking air activities with the RAF, as well as to foreign nationals flying with, or in conjunction with, the Royal Air Force, for an act of valour, courage or devotion to duty that was occasioned whilst flying but not in active operations against the enemy.

The ribbon comprises a 32 mm band with diagonal stripes of crimson and white, running at an angle of 45 degrees from left to right. When only the ribbon is worn, a silver rosette is applied to denote the award of a Bar.

GB.D014 The Conspicuous Gallantry Medal [Flying] — 15 January 1943

The obverse design of this Medal comprises a crowned head of George VI, with the inscription, 'GEOR-GIVS VI G.D.BR: OMN:REX ET INDIAE IMP'. Below the truncation of the head, in small raised capitals, are the initials 'PM' for the designer and engraver Percy Metcalfe.

The reverse has a raised edge line and flat field, on to which is placed a wreath of laurel leaves, the wreath being of a ragged or untidy type with a double bow at the bottom. At the apex of the wreath, which is open, is placed a Victorian crown. In the wreath is a three line inscription formed in small raised capitals, 'FOR, CONSPICUOUS, GALLANTRY'. Beneath the inscription is placed, just above the base of the wreath, a small pellet with side strokes. The Medal is issued named, being engraved in plain capital letters, without serifs. This is accompanied by the abbreviated rank and number. However, the rank is usually omitted in the case of awards rendered to warrant officers. 111 Medals were awarded during the period of the Second World War. The Medal has not been awarded on a

second occasion, hence no Bars have been issued.

This Medal was an extension of its naval counterpart to reward RAF warrant officers and below as well as Army personnel of equivalent rank who might, at any time, distinguish themselves by acts of conspicuous gallantry whilst flying in active operations against the enemy.

From the top of the medal is a ball and claw straight bar suspender, for attachment to the ribbon. The ribbon comprises a 32 mm band of pale blue, with dark blue edges that measure 3 mm, although some sources state that these blue edges sometimes measure between 4 mm to 5mm.

GB.D015 The Distinguished Flying Medal — 3 June 1918

This Medal was introduced on 3 June 1918 but the type that is relevant to the Second World War was introduced in 1938 and continued to be issued until 1949. The medal is oval with a raised edge that comprises a very small wreath of laurel leaves. These widen to the mid-point of the oval and then regress in the same proportion. The field is flat and on its centre is placed the bare head of George VI. The effigy employed is known as the coinage type with, beneath the truncation, in small raised capitals, 'HP' for T. Hugh Paget the designer and engraver. Round the edge is the inscription, 'GEORGIVS VI D:G:BR: OM N:REX F:D:IND:IMP:'.

The reverse was designed by the

Liverpool sculptor E. Carter Preston, his initials 'E.C.P.' (the 'C' has a small capital 'R' placed at the top curl), being found on a plinth beneath the right foot of the seated figure of Athena Nike. She rests on the engine cowling of a crashed biplane. Her right arm is held out horizontally and from the palm of her hand, poised for flight, is a hawk. Beneath her arm, in two lines, is the inscription, 'FOR, COURAGE' and above the hawk's wings, following the line of the wreath that forms the medal's edge, the date of institution, 1918.

The suspender comprises two small rosettes, one on the obverse and one on the reverse, which facilitate the attachment of the suspender to the body of the medal. This is

Above *Obverse The Distinguished Flying Medal George VI First type (GB.D015)*

accomplished by a rivet that runs through the centre or stamens of the flower. A stem rises with a circular lined finial. From this, on either side, is a pair of wings finished identically on the obverse and reverse. These have individual lines of fletching. The wings have an upturned tip on to which is placed a ball, through which runs the bar for the ribbon to run under. The Medal is issued named, this being found on the edge. In this case, the edge is slightly rounded and the name, rank and serial number, as well as the branch, are engraved in small capitals.

To denote the award of a second Medal, a Bar is placed on the ribbon and is identical to that employed on the Distinguished Flying Cross

(GB.D012), the Air Force Cross (GB.D013) and the Air Force Medal (GB.D016).

The Bar is flat with a central spine running the full length horizontally. On the middle of the bar is a flying air force eagle, looking to the right. The reverse of the bar is flat and at either end at 90 degrees is a return that forms a box. These returns have a semicircular top and bottom, through which is placed a small hole. This type of bar is known as the slip-on type and, as its name suggests, is simply slipped over the ribbon of the medal. On to the flat reverse, the date of the award of the Bar is inscribed. During the Second World War, 6,637 Medals, sixty first Bars and one second Bar were awarded.

The medal was to reward non-commissioned officers and men of the Royal Air Force and could subsequently be conferred on the equivalent ranks of the Army and Navy who were undertaking air activities with the RAF, as well as to foreign nationals flying with, or in conjunction with, the Royal Air Force for an act of valour, courage or devotion to duty that was occasioned whilst flying in active operations against the enemy. It was considered that the completion of forty operations against the enemy in bombing operations counted for the award of the medal as a recognition for devotion to duty.

The ribbon comprises a 32 mm band with alternate diagonal stripes of violet and white, running at an angle of 45 degrees from left to right. When only the ribbon is worn, to denote the award of a Bar a silver rosette is applied.

GB.D016 The Air Force Medal — 3 June 1918

The Medal was introduced on 3 June 1918 but the type that is relevant to the Second World War was introduced in 1938 and continued to be issued until 1949. The medal is oval with a raised edge that comprises a very small wreath of laurel leaves. These widen to the mid-point of the oval and then regress in the same proportion. The field is flat and on its centre is placed the bare head of George VI. The effigy that is employed is known as the coinage type with, beneath the truncation, in small raised capitals, 'HP' for T. Hugh Paget the designer and engraver. Round the edge is the inscription, 'GEORGIVS VI D:G:BR:OM N:REX F:D:IND:IMP:'.

The reverse was designed by the Liverpool sculptor E. Carter Preston, his initials 'E.C.P.' (the 'C' again has a small capital 'R' placed at the top curl) being found just in front of the hawk's claws and the wreath. The design is of Hermes standing on the back of a hawk, flying to the left. Hermes bends forwards holding a wreath in his right hand and a staff in his left. Behind the hawk's left wing and mid-point of the oval, is the date of institution, 1918. (Incidentally, this design follows the theme of the design of the central boss of the Air Force Cross (GB.D013) which, in that case, is without the date.)

The suspender comprises two small rosettes, one on the obverse and one on the reverse, which facilitate its attachment to the body of the medal. This is accomplished by means of a rivet that runs through the centre or stamens of the flower. A stem rises with a circular lined finial. From this, on either side, is a pair of wings finished identically on the obverse and reverse. These have individual lines of fletching. The wings have an upturned tip on to which is placed a ball, through which runs the bar for the ribbon to run under. The Medal is issued named, this being found on the edge. In this case, the edge is slightly rounded and the name, rank and serial number, as well as the branch, are engraved in small capitals.

To denote the award of a second Medal, a Bar identical to that employed on the Distinguished Flying Cross (GB.D012), the Air Force Cross (GB.D013) and the Distinguished Flying Medal (GB.D015) is placed on the ribbon. In the Second World War, 259 Medals were awarded but no Bars.

The Medal was to reward non-commissioned officers and men of the Royal Air Force and could subsequently be conferred on the equivalent ranks of the Army and Navy who were undertaking air activities with the RAF, as well as to foreign nationals flying with, or in conjunction with, the Royal Air Force for an act of valour, courage or devotion to duty that was occasioned whilst flying in non-active operations against the enemy.

The ribbon comprises a 32 mm band with alternate diagonal stripes of crimson and white, running at an angle of 45 degrees from left to right. When only the ribbon is worn, a silver rosette is applied to denote the award of a Bar.

Insignia of the various Commands of the RAF

The brevets described in the following text have changed due to the conditions that prevailed during the Second World War and to the individual importance placed on new skills that were developed as flying became more scientific. Development of larger and more powerful aeroplanes, and the ever-increasing demands on the skills of the electrical engineers to develop radar and radio telegraphy resulting from the speed of developments in electronics, particularly in Bomber Command, were meteoric.

The brevets that the aircrew were awarded were held in the highest esteem, even though they were only embroidered patches. There are two basic forms of nearly all of the insignia, the type worn on the flying blouse which was constructed in white and brown cotton sewn on to a dark blue or black melton backing, and a gold bullion-embroidered version which was worn on the dress uniform but was the same basic design. Again, these were embroidered on to a dark blue melton backing which was cut to the general shape of the outline of the whole of the insignia. There are many variations in the designs of the badges, both thread-embroidered and bullion-worked. This should not be considered unusual, considering

Below *Squadron Leader Fox [as a Sergeant] at the right of the picture with other members of Number 83 Squadron circa February 1941 at Scampton. The picture clearly shows various Wings, on obviously new uniforms.*

the number of badges produced during the period of the war and the countries in which they were manufactured. In this work I have only tried to identify the basic style used and its approximate introduction into service. A fine line as to exactly when a badge came on stream is hard to determine (unlike the case of Germany, when the introduction of the Swastika gives at least one defined date). In the case of the gold bullion wings it is not unusual to find certain parts finished in silver. The exact

reasoning behind this is unknown to this author, but in the case of the half wings, it is possible that the manufacturer was trying to enhance the appearance of the initials to make recognition easier. The thread-embroidered wings can be found either flat, semi-padded or thickly padded with the threads varying from slightly off-white to a very light bronze. In the case of those purchased by the individual, the pocket dictated the quality of the badge.

GB.A001 RAF Pilots' Wings — 1 April 1918
GB.A001b RAF Pilots' Wings (Bullion)

These were introduced on 1 April 1918 to replace those of the Royal Flying Corps and have remained basically unaltered, except for the addition of a queen's crown in 1952 which took place on the accession of Queen Elizabeth II to the throne of England. The wings changed from those of a swift, which had been employed by the RFC, to those of an eagle, and comprise a pair of wings that butt up to an open leafed laurel wreath. The wings on either side are identical, each consisting of an upper line of fletching which is solid embroidered. Beneath this is another line made up of individual feathers that are not very pronounced, numbering nine in total. Beneath this is a lower line of individual fletching, that starts at the wingtip with long feathers, the size of which reduces progressively from the tip to the wreath, there being normally ten in this lower row.

Above *RAF Pilots' Wings (GB.A001). Squadron Leader Fox's own Wings.*

The wreath comprises two laurel branches that overlap at the base and have five leaves on each side of each branch and one at the tip, making 22 leaves in total in the complete wreath. The centre has the monogram, 'R.A.F.' and the void at the apex of the wreath is filled with the crown. The embroidery is of white or off-white cotton thread for the monogram, wings and crown and brown for the wreath. The whole is executed on a dark blue or black melton cloth backing. The wings can also be encountered either in a semi-padded or very padded form. An incidental but, I consider, very interesting point was that the recipient purchased additional pairs from stores or tailors and uniform outfitters. The example shown is that of Squadron Leader Fox which was removed from his number 1 tunic after his death on the night of 24/25 October 1942. Still on the reverse was the hand written price label, 3/6d (in decimal currency that is $17\frac{1}{2}$ pence). The wings measure 98 mm wingtip to wingtip and 36 mm from the base of the wreath to the tip of the crown. It is worn above the left breast pocket, above any ribbons or decorations.

GB.A002 RAF Observers' Wing — September 1915
GB.A002b RAF Observers' Wing (Bullion)

This badge remained unaltered from its inception in 1915 until it was superseded in 1942 by the RAF Navigators' Wing (GB.A006) and comprises an embroidered oval 'O' which has chain stitch on its inner and outer edges. From the left hand side of the 'O' emanates an upswept wing. The example examined has thirteen lines of fletching that run horizontally. It is embroidered in white cotton thread on to a blue melton backing and was worn above the left breast pocket, above any ribbons or decorations.

Above *RAF Observers' Wing (GB.A002)* (Margaret Nobbs)

GB.A003 RAF Air Gunners' Wing — December 1939
GB.A003b RAF Air Gunners' Wing (Bullion)

This badge was introduced in December 1939 to replace the winged bullet that had been worn previously to identify air gunners. This new brevet consisted of a wreath similar to that found on the Pilots' Wings (GB.A001) but, in this case, not so tightly curved. The apex is open and there is no crown. The centre of the wreath contains the initials 'AG' in capital letters, for air gunner. The wreath is embroidered in brown cotton thread, the wing and 'AG' in off-white cotton thread, all executed on a blue melton cloth backing. It was worn above the left breast pocket, above any ribbons or decorations.

Right *RAF Air Gunners' Wing (GB.A003)* (Margaret Nobbs)

GB.A004 RAF Flight Engineers' Wing — 1941
GB.A004b RAF Flight Engineers' Wing (Bullion)

This badge was introduced to reward the skills of the new 'on board' engineers, who were becoming ever more increasingly important in monitoring the engines' performance in flight. It was born out of the technical advances in aero-engineering. Originally the pilot, then the observer, was the most important person in an aircraft. With the development of the war and, highly sophisticated aeroplanes, the emphasis changed to the concept of a crew of equal partners, a team that delivered a plane carrying a cargo of bombs to a target and, hopefully, back to base again. From 1941 the importance of 'crewing up' was brought into being.

This badge consisted of a wreath with, at its centre, the initials in capital letters, 'FE', for flight engineer. From the wreath was a single wing. The wreath was executed in brown cotton thread and the wing and initials in off-white. It was worn above the left breast pocket, above any ribbons or decorations.

GB.A005 RAF Radio Operators' Wing — 1941
GB.A005b RAF Radio Operators' Wing (Bullion)

This comprised a similar wreath with, in the centre, 'RO' in capitals for radio operator, with a similar single wing. The wing and the initials are in off-white cotton thread, the wreath is again in brown on a blue melton base. It was worn above the left breast pocket, above any ribbons or decorations.

Right *RAF Radio Operators' Wing (GB.A005)* (Margaret Nobbs)

GB.A006 RAF Navigators' Wing — 1942
GB.A006b RAF Navigators' Wing (Bullion)

As flying duties became more complex due to the technical advances that were being developed in aerial warfare, in March 1942 the bombers began to receive new navigational aids. The first of these was Gee that began to be installed in that month, followed by Oboe in December and H2S in January 1943. The Observers' Badge (GB.A002) had been adopted in 1915 to recognize what was considered at the time a more important position in the two-seater planes than that of the pilot who commanded it. The pilot functioned primarily as a taxi driver for the observer, whose job it was to observe the enemy and to direct the plane to the target. The new navigational aids required new skills, so the new badge was introduced in 1942 to denote and reward the acquisition of these.

It takes the form of a wreath with, at its centre, a capital 'N' for navigator, with a single wing. The wreath is finished in brown cotton thread and the initials and wing are executed in off-white cotton thread, all embroidered on to a blue melton backing. It

was worn above the left breast pocket, above any ribbons or decorations.

Above *RAF Navigators' Wing (GB.A006)* (Margaret Nobbs)

Below *RAF Navigators' Wing [Bullion] (GB.A006b)* (Margaret Nobbs)

GB.A007 RAF Flight Engineers' Wing — 1942
GB.A007b RAF Flight Engineers' Wing (Bullion)

This badge was introduced in 1942 and comprises a similar wreath to that found on GB.A004 but with the capital 'F' being omitted, thus just leaving the 'E' in the centre for engineer. A single wing of the same design is placed in the same relative position. The wreath was produced in brown cotton thread and the wing and initial in off-white cotton thread on to a blue melton cloth backing. The reasoning for reorganizing the badge is unknown to the author but this is the most commonly encountered version employed during the Second World War. It was worn above the left breast pocket, above any ribbons or decorations.

Above *RAF Flight Engineers' Wing (GB.A007)* (Margaret Nobbs)

GB.A008 RAF Bomb Aimers' Wing — 1942
GB.A008b RAF Bomb Aimers' Wing (Bullion)

This badge, like the others introduced in 1942, recognized the importance of the individual team members who went into the formation of a harmonious crew. The bomb aimer had the singularly important task of guiding the plane into the target on the final bombing run. It was his expertise that delivered the punch that finally defeated German industry and determined if the flight had been successful or not. The capability of bomb aimers is illustrated by an event that took place on the night

Above *RAF Bomb Aimers' Wing (GB.A008)* (Margaret Nobbs)

Above *Reverse The Distinguished Flying Medal George VI First type (GB.D015). The two eyelets were placed on the suspender for the suspension of the medal by means of a silver chain, when Mrs Fox visited a reunion in Canada.*

Above right *Obverse The Distinguished Flying Medal George VI First type (GB.DO15)*

Right *Obverse 1939–1945 Star (GB.D017)*

Above left *Obverse The Atlantic Star (GB.D018)*

Above *Obverse The Air Crew Europe Star (GB.D019). This is the Star awarded to Squadron Leader Fox.*

Left *The Africa Star (GB.D020)*

Above *Obverse The Pacific Star (GB.D021)*

Above right *Obverse The Burma Star (GB.D022)*

Right *Obverse The Italy Star (GB.D023)*

Above left *Obverse The France and Germany Star (GB.D024)*

Above *Reverse The Defence Medal (GB.D025)*

Left *Obverse The War Medal (GB.D026) with Mentioned in Despatches (GB.D027) on the ribbon.*

of 23/24 May 1943 on the return flight from an attack on Dortmund in a Wellington of 431 Squadron. After having been coned by searchlights and sustaining several hits by flak fragments, the rear gunner reported to the pilot that he thought the aircraft was on fire. The pilot twice put the aircraft into a steep dive to break out of the searchlight's cone. This effect was not achieved. There followed some confusion over whether the pilot gave an order to bale out, but the pilot seemed not to be in doubt and actually left the aircraft. Sergeant S.N. Sloan, the bomb aimer, took over the controls and was able to shake off the searchlights eventually. The navigator, Sergeant G.C.W. Parslow, and wireless operator, J.B.G. Bailey, were still aboard with Sergeant Sloan. He flew the aircraft back to England and effected a perfect landing at Cranwell. His skill was immediately recognized by his being commissioned and being sent to a pilot training course and being awarded the Conspicuous Gallantry Medal, GB.D014. The wireless operator

Above *RAF Bomb Aimers' Wing [Bullion] (GB.A008b)* (Margaret Nobbs)

received the DFC (GB.D012) and the navigator received the DFM (GB.D015).

The badge consists of an open work wreath with a capital 'B' for bomb aimer and a single wing in the same relative position to that found on the other badges. The wreath was executed in brown cotton thread and the initials and wing in off-white cotton thread, embroidered on a blue melton backing. It was worn above the left breast pocket, above any ribbons or decorations.

GB.A009 RAF Signallers' Wing — 1944
GB.A009b RAF Signallers' Wing (Bullion)

This badge was introduced in 1944 to acknowledge the broader use of wireless and radar. The official title was actually Signaller, even though

this conjures up the illusion and impression of semaphore. This title (again this is purely conjecture) could have been brought in just to confuse enemy intelligence as to the true importance of the operative. The badge consisted, as with the others, of an open work wreath with, at its centre, a capital 'S', with a single wing in the same relative position. The wreath was executed in brown cotton thread, while the 'S' and wing were in off-white cotton thread on a blue melton backing. It was worn above the left breast pocket, above any ribbons or decorations.

Above *RAF Signallers' Wing (GB.A009)* (Margaret Nobbs)

GB.A010 RAF Wireless Operator Air Gunners' Wing — 1944
GB.A010b RAF Wireless Operator Air Gunners' Wing (Bullion)

This badge was introduced at the same time as GB.A009 and took account of the significant change in the role of the signaller and the dual role of the air gunner in certain crews. It is only fair to say that, during the war the expertise of the bomber crews and their willingness to adapt and improvise, often at great risk to their own personal safety, brought about the advances in techniques of aerial bombardment that turned what had been a random hit or miss affair into a highly sophisticated science.

The badge comprises an open work wreath with the initials, in capital letters 'WAG' at its centre, to represent wireless operator air gunner. A single wing is placed in the relevant position. The wreath is produced in brown cotton thread while the initial and wing are in off-white

thread, executed on a blue melton cloth backing. It was worn above the left breast pocket, above any ribbons or decorations.

Below *RAF Wireless Operator Air Gunners' Wing (GB.A010)* (Margaret Nobbs)

GB.A011 RAF Parachute Training Instructors' Wing — 1945
GB.A011b RAF Parachute Training Instructor's Wing (Bullion)

There is some little doubt as to the date of institution of this badge. It is in some references placed as being introduced shortly after World War 2 and in some circles, in the closing stages of the war. On the advice of the eminent RAF expert Margaret Nobbs, who has been of the greatest help (the majority of the RAF wings illustrated in this section being from her unique collection), I have included it.

It consists of an open work wreath with, instead of initials, an open parachute, with the single wing indicative of aircrew, placed in the same relative position. This was the first

Above *RAF Parachute Training Instructors' Wing (GB.A011)* (Margaret Nobbs)

time that this category of RAF personnel was formally awarded aircrew status. It was worn above the left breast pocket, above any ribbons or decorations.

GB.A012 RAF Pathfinders' Badge — 1942-1945

The Pathfinder Force was set up in August 1942 to mark targets for the bombers who followed in their wake. For some time, Bomber Command had been using 'raid leaders' in attempts to improve target finding. Some crews in most squadrons, by natural ability, survival and experience were found to have a greater success rate than others. The obvious conclusion in certain quarters was to gather those crews together into one force and this concept had been kick-

ing around the Air Ministry since late 1941. It was the brainchild of Group Captain S.O. Bufton and during the next months, against criticism that forming an elite group within Bomber Command might produce disharmony, the concept of a target force was nurtured. Bufton gained the support of his fellow staff officers at the Air Ministry, but when the idea was put to 'Bomber' Harris in February 1942, when he took over command of Bomber Command, he

Above *RAF Pathfinders' Badge (GB.A012)*
(Margaret Nobbs)

was violently opposed on both the aforementioned grounds and his strongly held belief that experienced crews should stay with their squadrons to give example and to lead the inexperienced new crews. The opposition continued during the year with Bufton coming up with various conciliatory alternatives. However, the wrangling became so intense, that Sir Charles Portal made the enlightened decision to take the advice of his own staff, as opposed to that of his field commanders, and ordered Harris to inaugurate the force. Harris, still opposed, rejected the original name and christened it the Pathfinder Force. Thus, on 11 August 1942, the order was given for the creation of the force. Even the appointment of the new commander was fraught with difficulty but eventually the distinguished Australian Wing Com-

mander D.C.T Bennett was chosen. Bennett located his headquarters at Wyton airfield in Huntingdonshire in 1943, then at Castle Hill House in Huntingdon. The satellite aerodrome of Upwood in Cambridgeshire was also used for Pathfinder and reconnaissance operations. Bennett remained in command until the end of the Second World War.

To recognize the skills of those crews assigned to Pathfinder duties, a small metal badge was produced in brass, which comprises a forage cap eagle but without the royal crown. This consists of an eagle in flight with horizontally outstretched wings and head extended. The tail feathers are splayed and pointed downwards with the talons slightly exposed under the body. This badge is found with the eagle's head facing to the left, its shape and the fletching patterns of the body varying, due to manufacturing differences. The badge is also found with the eagle flying in the opposite direction. The reason for this mirrored badge is unknown to the author. The reverse has two screw posts on to which is placed a screw nut for attachment to the uniform. It was worn on the left breast pocket, 4.8 mm below the seam.

GB.A013 RAF Operational Tours Badge — 12 August 1943-1945

By 1942 it was considered necessary to recognize the crews with a long standing record of flying operations. In conjunction with the Pathfinder

Badge (GB.A012), it was decided to give an outward show of these achievements. 'Bomber' Harris felt it essential to keep up the morale of his senior crews, thus strengthening the morale of the newcomers. This is illustrated by Squadron Leader Fox's last flight, for in fact the new pilot, Sergeant Henry Frederick Wood, had not been on the station long enough to take his kit from the guardroom before, as Fox put it, he went on a continental holiday to see the Alps. He was killed in the air attack on 'D' for Donald that terminated the flight over France. This situation of young crew members being killed on their first operation was not an uncommon occurrence. The Luftwaffe's night fighters had become very effective by the autumn of 1942.

The badge consists of an oval 'O' with the centre voided, with a pair of wings joined on to either side. They consist of eight lines of horizontal fletching with an overall measurement of 41 mm horizontally and 10 mm vertically. It is constructed of brass, and gilded. The reverse has, like the Pathfinders' Badge (GB.A012), two screw posts with a nut attached to each to allow the badge to be fixed to the uniform, being worn on the left breast pocket, 4.8 mm below the seam. If the Pathfinders' Badge GB.A012 was held, this badge was worn directly below it.

To mark further tours of operation, a bar was fixed horizontally below the 'O', thus the addition of one bar represented the completion of two tours of operation. This was extended up to three bars which represented four tours. A tour of operation was considered to consist of forty operational flights.

GB.A014 Air Transport Auxiliary Pilots' Wings — 11 September 1939
GB.A014b Air Transport Auxiliary Pilots' Wings (Bullion)

This badge is found both in beige silk and gold bullion wire. The general design for both of these badges is identical, but the actual fletching, on close examination, has a different appearance. This is true for the three types of badges described in GB.A014, GB.A015 and GB.A016, each with their individual bullion versions but for simplification I will describe the badges as one type and just note the variation to the fletching

Below *RAF Air Transport Auxiliary Pilots' Wings [Bullion] (GB.A014b)* (Margaret Nobbs)

Above *RAF Air Transport Auxiliary Pilots'*
Wings [Bullion] (GB.A014b) Variation
(Margaret Nobbs)

at the end. The badge is very rare, the bullion type seeming to be the brevet that was most usually worn.

The Air Transport Auxiliary was formed on 11 September 1939. It was under the command of the Ministry of Aircraft Production but was administered by the British Overseas Airways Corporation (BOAC) so that personnel were able to land at neutral countries' airports without breaking the neutrality treaty and thus being detained and their aircraft impounded. In fact, a regular air service was in operation between Scotland and Sweden, operated by BOAC, which flew converted Mosquitoes in civil colours to transport ball bearings for the war effort. Their speed rendered them uncatchable by the Luftwaffe. This practice was to cause the Nazi government much annoyance and Sweden was put under great diplomatic pressure to resist the flights. The personnel were also employed in ferrying aircraft within the UK as well as from America. The organization was absorbed by Transport Command in 1943 but its personnel continued to wear the

badge until the end of the war. This was to uphold the non-military stance, when such flights were necessary.

The badge comprises an oval, constructed of two lines of twisted bullion wire. The centre has a large 'T' with, on either side, a small capital 'A'. The oval has a wing on either side, formed at the upper edge with a single line of twisted bullion wire that matches that employed on the central 'O'. Beneath this is a line of fletching with diagonal stitching running downward from left to right on the left-hand wing and the opposite direction on the right-hand wing. This mirror appearance is continued across the design of the wing. Beneath the line is a black cotton outline stitch. The next line of fletching comprises seven individual feathers with pronounced 'V' tips, outlined with black thread. The lower line has eight individual feathers, again with pronounced 'V' tips and outlined with black thread. The bullion embroidery of these feathers is in the opposite direction to that of those above. The whole of the badge is worked on to a black melton backing.

The silk-embroidered type was executed in beige thread and has an upper line of fletching with, beneath, ten individual feathers which are machine-embroidered and run uninterrupted from the upper line of the wing and form the lower line. The 'O' at the centre is formed solid, as opposed to the two lines in the bullion form. It is also embroidered on a black melton cloth backing.

Both were worn on the left breast of the tunic above the ribbons or any decorations.

GB.A015 Air Transport Auxiliary Flight Engineers' Wing — 11 September 1939
GB.A015b Air Transport Auxiliary Flight Engineers' Wing (Bullion)

This badge is found both in beige silk and gold bullion wire, and as with GB.A014 the general design for either is identical although the actual fletching, on close examination, has a different appearance.

It was introduced at the same time as the ATA Pilots' Wings and the only difference in their design is that the oval 'O' has only one wing, which is positioned to the left. The badge was to recognize flight engineers and is extremely rare, as it is estimated that there were only 500 flight engineers in the organization. They were worn on the left breast of the tunic, above the ribbons or any other decorations.

Above *RAF Air Transport Auxiliary Flight Engineers' Wing [Bullion] (GB.A015b)* (Margaret Nobbs)

GB.A016 Air Transport Auxiliary Engineers' Wing — 11 September 1939
GB.A016b Air Transport Auxiliary Engineers' Wing (Bullion)

This badge is also found both in beige silk and gold bullion wire and is identical to the two previous ones (GB.A015 and GB.A015b), with the addition of a horizontal two-bladed propeller placed directly above the oval. It is also very rare. It was worn on the left breast of the tunic, above the ribbons or any other decorations.

GB.A017 RAF Ferry Command Pilots' Wings — 14 June 1941-25 March 1943

The shortage of qualified pilots and the need to transport aircraft, not only from their places of production in Great Britain but also from America and Canada, placed a great strain on the RAF. This strain was alleviated, to a certain extent, by the Air Transport Auxiliaries, the use of experienced pilots who were basically too old for combat and of women pilots becoming essential to the war effort. With the institution of Ferry Command a pilots' wing was necessary, and this consists of a circle made up of circular stitching. The central field thus produced has vertical lines of bullion on to which are embroidered the monogram 'R.A.F.' in a stylized form. From either side was a pair of wings formed in the same method as that employed in GB.A014b. One point of interest is that the bullion wire is executed as a mirror image of that found on the relevant wing of the Air Transport Auxiliary Pilots' Wings. Surmounting the 'O' is a crown of the astral type. Beneath the 'O' is a panel which has an outline similar to that of the 'O' and the same vertical, lined field.

Above *RAF Ferry Command Pilots' Wings (GB.A017)* (Margaret Nobbs)

This panel or banner is separated from the 'O' by approximately 1 mm. The wings, circle, crown, monogram and the outline to the banner are executed in gold bullion wire. The banner's field is embroidered in yellow silk but contains no inscription. The field of the circle is blue. The whole design is embroidered on to a dark blue wool background, and the badge measures 87 mm horizontally, wingtip to wingtip, and 34 mm vertically.

The brevet was worn on the left breast of the tunic, above the ribbons or any other decorations.

GB.A018 RAF Ferry Command Engineers' Wing — 14 June 1941-25 March 1943

This badge is of a similar design to the Pilots' Wings (GB.A017), with the exception that the right-hand wing is omitted. Thus it consists of a circle made up of circular stitching. The central field has vertical lines of bullion on which are embroidered the monogram 'R.A.F.' in a stylized form. From the left side emanates a wing formed in the same method as that employed in GB.A015b. One point of interest is that the bullion wire is executed in the same manner as that found on the relevant wing of the Air Transport Auxiliary Flight Engineers' Wing (GB.A015b). Surmounting the 'O' is a crown of the astral type. Beneath the 'O' is a panel which has an outline similar to that of the 'O' and the same vertical, lined field. This panel or banner is separated from the 'O' by approximately 1 mm. The wings, circle, crown, monogram and the outline to the banner are executed in gold bullion wire. The banner's field is embroidered in yellow silk but contains no inscription. The field of the circle is produced in blue and the whole design is embroidered on to a dark blue wool background. The badge measures 54 mm horizontally, wingtip to wingtip, and 34 mm vertically.

The brevet was worn on the left breast of the tunic, above the ribbons or any other decorations.

Above *RAF Ferry Command Engineers' Wing (GB.A018)* (Margaret Nobbs)

GB.A019 RAF Ferry Command Pilots' Wings — 14 June 1941-1945

Why a second and different set of Ferry Command Pilots' Wings to GB.A017 was considered necessary is unknown to this author, but may have had something to do with neutrality treaties, as discussed in the Air Transport Auxiliary section (GB.A014). The wings, however, conform to the same general overall theme with, at the centre, an embroidered circle surmounted by an astral crown. A banner is positioned beneath the circle but in this case it has the circle's edge as the top line, instead of being a separate piece. From either side of the 'O' emanate a pair of wings. The upper fletch has the appearance of a cucumber, with an outline of bullion wire. Beaneath is a row of four individual feathers, with ellipsed ends outlined with black cotton thread. Beneath this is another row of six feathers, again with the ellipsed tips and outlined with black

Above *RAF Ferry Command Pilots' Wings (GB.A019)* (Margaret Nobbs)

cotton thread. This gives a more sleek and aerodynamic appearance to these wings as opposed to their counterparts. The RAF monogram is worked on to a blue silk field, the banner also being executed in blue, and has the inscription, 'FERRY COMMAND', in small capitals, worked in bullion. The overall colour is of gold bullion.

The brevet was worn on the left breast of the tunic, above any ribbons or decorations.

GB.A020 RAF Ferry Command Engineers' Wing — 14 June 1941-1945

As in the previous entry, this is a second badge awarded for the same basic qualifying skills as GB.A018, and the same reasons may apply, or it might be a simple difference between manufacturers. Again it conforms to the same general overall theme with, at the centre, an embroidered circle surmounted by an astral crown. A banner is positioned beneath the circle but in this case it has the circle's edge as the top line, instead of being a separate piece. From the left-hand side of the 'O' emanates a single wing. The upper fletch has the appearance of a cucumber, with an outline of bullion wire. Beneath is a row of four individual feathers, with ellipsed ends outlined with black cotton thread. Beneath this is another row of six feathers, again with the ellipsed tips and outlined with black cotton

Above *RAF Ferry Command Engineers' Wing (GB.A020)* (Margaret Nobbs)

thread. The RAF monogram is worked on to a blue silk field, and the banner is also executed in blue with the inscription, 'FERRY COMMAND', in small capitals, worked in bullion.

The brevet was worn on the left breast of the tunic, above any ribbons or decorations.

GB.A021 RAF Transport Command Pilots' Wings — 25 March 1943-1945

At the beginning of March 1943 it was decided to reorganize RAF Ferry Command into RAF Transport Command, which came into being on 25 March 1943. A new brevet was introduced to denote this change. It takes the general theme of its counterpart, having as its central motif a circle formed by two rows of twisted bullion wire similar to that of the ATA Pilots Wings' (GB.A014B).

The field in this case is of royal blue velvet or wool, on which is placed the letters 'R.A.F.', again in twisted bullion wire. From either side emanate a pair of wings which have an upper line of similar twisted bullion. The 'cucumber' is executed in diagonal bullion thread and outlined with similar twisted bullion. Beneath this is a second line of four individual feathers outlined similarly. The third and lower line is outlined in black cotton thread. From this, and running beneath the circle, is a banner, whose upper line is formed by the circle's lower one. The ends and lower line are formed likewise by twisted bullion wire. The field is of dark blue velvet or wool, on to which is worked in bullion wire in small capital letters, 'TRANSPORT COMMAND'. Above the central circle is an elongated astral crown. The badge measures horizontally wingtip to wingtip 83 mm and vertically from the bottom of the banner to the top of the crown 35 mm. In this case the badge

is worked in silver bullion wire on to a dark blue backing.

It was worn on the left breast of the uniform above any ribbons or decorations.

Above *RAF Transport Command Pilots' Wings with Squadron Number (GB.A021v)* (Margaret Nobbs)

GB.A021v RAF Transport Command Pilots' Wings with Squadron Number

The purpose of this badge is identical to its predecessor's but takes into account the individual squadron to which the pilot belonged. It is, again, of the same general appearance as the former Pilots' Badge (GB.A021) but with these significant differences. The central 'O' is smaller and more rounded with the 'A' of the 'R.A.F.' monogram being larger, in a similar manner to that embroidered in the monogram of the ATA. The wings curve down to the tip whereas the former one has an upturned end. The wings' second rows of fletching are in five as opposed to four individual feathers. Similarly, in the lower line there are six as opposed to five individual feathers. The banner runs under the circle as in the previous badge but, in this case, starts from the underside of the lower line of fletch-

Above *RAF Transport Command Pilots' Wings with Squadron Number (GB.A021v)* (Margaret Nobbs)

ing. This gives rise to the increase in the number of feathers in the second and third rows. On to the banner is, in bullion wire, in small capitals, 'A.T.C.' and the squadron number. The squadrons that made up the Command were numbered 24, 44, 45, 46, 47, 112, 113, 179, 216, 229, 271, 510 and 511. The wings measure 75 mm horizontally, wingtip to wingtip, and 34 mm vertically from the base of the banner to the top of the crown.

The badge was worn on the left breast of the uniform above the ribbons or any decorations.

GB.A022 RAF Transport Command Engineers' Wing — 25 March 1943-1945

This badge was to be the outward show of engineers employed in Transport Command and comprised a single wing identical to GB.A021. It was also brought into existence when Ferry Command was reorganized into RAF Transport Command on 25 March 1943. The new brevet takes the general theme of its counterpart, having as its central motif a circle formed by two rows of twisted bullion wire similar to that of the ATA Pilots' Wings (GB.A014B). The field in this case is of royal blue velvet or wool, on to which the letters 'R.A.F.' are placed, again in twisted bullion wire. From the left-hand side emanates a single wing which has an upper line of similar twisted bullion. The 'cucumber' is executed in diagonal bullion thread and outlined with sim-

ilar twisted bullion. Beneath this is a second line of four individual feathers outlined similarly. The third and lower line is outlined in black cotton thread. From this and running beneath the circle is a banner, whose upper line is formed by the circle's lower one. The ends and lower line are formed likewise by twisted bullion wire. The field is of dark blue velvet or wool, on to which is worked in bullion wire in small capital letters, 'TRANSPORT COMMAND'. Above the central circle is an elongated astral crown. In this case the badge is worked in silver bullion wire on to a dark blue backing.

It was worn on the left breast of the uniform above any ribbons or decorations.

GB.A022v RAF Transport Command Engineers' Wing with Squadron Number

The purpose of this badge is identical to its predecessor's but takes into account the individual squadron to which the engineer belonged. It is, again, of the same general appearance as the former Engineers' Badge (GB.A022) but with these significant

differences. The central 'O' in this badge is smaller and more rounded with the 'A' of the 'R.A.F.' monogram being larger, in a similar manner to that embroidered in the monogram of the ATA. The wing curves down to the tip whereas the former one has an upturned end. The wing's second row of fletching consists of five individual feathers instead of four. In the lower line there are six individual feathers as opposed to five. The banner runs under the circle as in the previous badge but, in this case, starts from the underside of the lower line of fletch-

ing. This gives rise to the increase in the number of feathers in the second and third rows. On the banner is, in bullion wire, in small capitals, 'A.T.C.' and the squadron number. The squadrons that made up the Command are enumerated under GB.A021V.

GB.A023 Special Forces Pilots' Wings — 1942-1945

Special Forces Wings, as the name implies, were for the specially trained units that fought the clandestine war. This involved the piloting of Lysanders and other aircraft into occupied territory to reinforce resistance groups, to take in agents and to bring them out and all the other exceptionally difficult and dangerous tasks that this force was employed to undertake. I have encountered two distinct types, one of which has been attributed to flying personnel and the other to paratroopers. However, as they are basically homemade, the exact purpose of either of these badges may never be fully known.

The pilots' version comprises a pair of wings, identical to those of the RAF pilot (GB.A001) with, instead of the wreath, a circled hand which is of red wool, stitched to the relevant position. On to this is stitched in light blue cotton, in capital letters, 'S.F.'. It is executed on a dark blue wool backing and measures 109 mm horizontally wingtip to wingtip and 23 mm vertically.

The second version had the central circle in red, bearing in pale blue

Above RAF Special Forces Pilots' Wings (GB.A023) (Fred Stephens)

initials, executed in thread, 'S.F.'. The wings, however, are of a totally different configuration, having a top line of fletching running horizontally upwards and underlined with black thread. Beneath this are six individual feathers outlined with black thread. Beneath them is a further line which has five individual feathers, again picked out with black cotton thread. The wings at the central circle are attached by approximately 2 mm of fletching. This gives a very clear definition to the disc and the wings, which are grey-brown in colour.

This type of wing is attributed to the Jedburgh detachments, Anglo-US-French three-man teams parachuted into Normandy before and on D-Day to organize and co-ordinate the activities of the Resistance with the Allies' battle plan. Special Forces HQ was the headquarters which raised and trained these detachments. The French and American personnel of the triumvirate were the nationals mostly to have worn this type, the British retaining their usual parachute qualification wings by personal preference.

Both Special Forces wings were worn on the left breast of the service tunic above the ribbons or any decorations.

Campaign medals and stars for all Services, and the allies serving with those forces

The whole area of campaign stars and clasps is riddled with anomalies and pitfalls for the collector. Eight stars were produced in the end for British, Colonial and Commonwealth troops, together with the Defence Medal and the War Medal (GB.D025 and GB.D026). However, the Honours Committee decided in their infinite wisdom that no-one could receive more than five stars, plus the two medals, as appropriate. For this reason clasps were authorized, mirroring the practice of awarding bars to medals, but for participation in different campaigns, albeit that there are Army clasps awarded to be worn on the Africa Star (GB.D020). Thus a man could win the Atlantic Star (GB.D018) serving with Coastal Command, for example, but if he then went on to serve a European tour in bombers, say, he would get the France and Germany Clasp (GB.C009) to pin to the ribbon of his star. However, only one clasp could be pinned to any one ribbon, so if he then went on to serve in the Far East he might get the Burma Star (GB.D002), plus Pacific Clasp (GB.C007) or vice versa, depending upon when he became eligible for each.

Above *Pilot Officer Geoff Wollerton after his return from Germany, at RAF Uxbridge processing service records. The poster behind his head illustrates the ribbons of the campaign medals and stars.*

Far Eastern stars and clasps are included briefly in this section even though this book concentrates upon awards to personnel serving in or out of the United Kingdom, for one individual's complete set of decorations could include them. The listing of all the campaign stars that were awarded for all theatres of operations is included, because the unit to which the recipient was attached could have gained that award during his attachment to the unit while based in Great Britain. The engagement in another theatre of operations is easily explained by the example of a bomber crew that flew from a British airfield to bomb a target for example in Italy or Rumania, and then flew on to Malta or Gibraltar for refuelling and then were subsequently diverted to Egypt and then on to India. Hence, the Burma or Pacific Star could be awarded to the crew if the period of time spent in the Pacific theatre of operations qualified the person for the award of such a star.

It was not unusual to find high-ranking Generals or Squadron-Leaders travelling to various bases on a tour of inspection and prolonging their stay long enough to qualify them for that theatre of operation's star, giving rise to the expression, 'gong hunting'. This devalues these awards in the minds of many of their genuine recipients.

The fact that the government decided in its infinite wisdom not to award these stars and medals named, has made the collector's task of verifying groups nearly impossible, unless accompanied by a named medal or flying log book. It also affords the unscrupulous dealer the opportunity to make up groups to important people from rare decorations such as the Distinguished Flying Cross, [GB. D012], which has only the date of award on its reverse, with common-or-garden stars, thus enhancing their commercial value and selling the same group with as many verifying documents as are in his possession.

This practice, I must hasten to say, is not the sole prerogative of the unscrupulous dealer. Some collectors are far worse in their historical fabrications, as well as some recipients who have applied for replacement medals. One example that comes to mind is of a D.F.M., [GB. D015], that was sold and subsequently the recipient attempted to sell his second replacement 2 or 3 years later to the same dealer.

In some cases, when a veteran had been demobbed, he had to apply for the bestowal of his medals rather than being awarded them automatically. A case in point is my uncle, who had been a prisoner of war of the Japanese for five years. Upon his release, he was hospitalized in the Phillipines and America, serving the end of his tour in Canada where he was demobbed, and finally returned to the UK. After demob he received a letter asking him to state which stars he thought he was eligible for and to make a claim for their award. His comments are unprintable!

Yet another complication lies in the fact that the qualifying period serving in a particular theatre for a star or clasp varied, so some people who thought they were eligible ended up being disappointed. One of the reasons for the confusion here is that the qualifying period was totalled in 30-day 'months'.

The design of all eight stars is identical. They are six point, with a central boss. The arms of the star each have a raised central spine running to the line around the edge of the boss. There is an inner line forming a 'tramline', upon which is the raised relevant inscription. The field is finely pebbled and the central boss has a flat field, with the royal cypher of George VI upon it in two lines. Through this field, the 'tramline' and on to the upper arm of the star is the royal crown. The upper arm also has a protrusion, through which runs the ribbon ring. The reverse is flat and plain and each star measures 44 mm across its arms.

Index to campaign stars, clasps and medals

GB.D017 1939-1945 Star

This Star was to reward service in the Second World War between the dates of 3 September 1939 and 2 September 1945. Army and Navy personnel had the general qualification of six months in an operational area. The merchant navy had the same period of service, but with the requirement that a minimum of one voyage had been made through an operational area. The RAF aircrews had to complete two months' service in an operational area and to have been involved in flying operations against the enemy. RAF ground forces had to complete the six-month qualification period in an operational Army command. Service that was terminated by death or disability due to service, rendered the recipient eligible for the award of the Star. An award of a decoration, Mention in Despatches (GB.D027) or a King's Commendation (GB.C010) also qualified the recipient for the award of the Star.

The ribbon comprises three equal stripes of dark blue, red and light blue, to represent the Navy, Army and Air Force.

GB.C001 Battle of Britain Clasp

This bronze Clasp was sewn on to the ribbon of the 1939-1945 Star (GB.D017), by means of two small holes at either end of the bar. The bar has the inscription, 'BATTLE OF BRITAIN' and was to reward the crews of fighter aircraft who between 10 July and 31 October 1940 had taken part in the Battle of Britain. When only the ribbon was worn, a gilt rosette was attached. To qualify for the Clasp, the recipient must have been a member of a specific squadron and the flight interception unit. To have taken part in the battle unofficially or by accident, did not qualify the pilot or aircrew for the award of the bar.

Above *Battle of Britain Clasp (GB.C001)* (Spink & Son Ltd)

GB.D018 The Atlantic Star

This Star was to reward those who had fought in the Battle of the Atlantic between the qualifying periods of 3 September 1939 to 8 May 1945. The star has the inscription 'THE ATLANTIC STAR' placed in the 'tramlines' and was awarded for six months' service at sea. This was the same for both the Navy and the merchant navy but the actual areas differ. It was a prerequisite that the 1939–1945 Star (GB.D017), had been earned. In the case of the RAF the qualifying period was two months' service with an operational squadron. RAF and Army personnel serving with the Navy would qualify under the same conditions as their naval compatriots.

Service that was terminated by death or disability, rendered the recipient eligible for the award of the Star, as did the award of a decoration, Mention in Despatches (GB.D027) or a King's Commendation (GB.C010). Those qualifying for the Atlantic Star, the France and Germany Star (GB.D024) and the Air Crew Europe Star (GB.D019), were only awarded the Star they qualified for first and then the relevant Clasp to denote the second Star they had been awarded.

watered and shaded in blue, white and sea green, to represent the Royal Navy and the Atlantic Ocean.

GB.C002 Atlantic Clasp

This is identical to GB.C001 save for the inscription and is attached to the ribbon of the relevant star in the same manner.

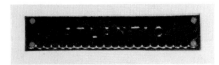

Above *The Atlantic Clasp (GB.C002)* (Spink & Son Ltd)

GB.D019 Air Crew Europe Star

This, of all the stars, is the most difficult to obtain. It was a prerequisite that the recipient had already been awarded the 1939-1945 Star (GB.D017) and had been involved in flying duties over Europe during the qualifying period of 3 September 1939 to 5 June 1944 and had not received the award of any other star for the same duty. Thus, the recipient must have completed four months as a member of an aircrew, with any two months qualifying, when operationally flying from a United Kingdom base. One bone of contention has

been that prisoners of war are not awarded the Star unless they had received the 1939-1945 Star (GB.D017), but service terminated by death or disability rendered a man eligible for the star.

The ribbon comprises a 32 mm band with a central 18 mm pale blue stripe. This is bounded on either side by a 2 mm yellow stripe, flanked by a black edge stripe that measures 4 mm. The colours emblematically represent the Air Force and the day and night flying operations.

GB.C003 Air Crew Europe Clasp

As GB.C002.

Right *Air Crew Europe Clasp (GB.C003)* (Spink & Son Ltd)

GB.D020 Africa Star

This Star was to reward those forces involved in North Africa, Abyssinia, Eritrea, Malta and Somaliland, the qualifying period being from 10 June 1940 to 12 May 1943, the latter being the day before the last enemy troops surrendered in Africa. It recognizes Wavell's brilliant campaigns which Churchill did not appreciate, relieving him of his command in November 1941. During his time as Commander in Chief in the Middle East from July 1939 to November 1941, the Italian 10th Army had advanced into Egypt on 13 September 1940 and in five days were sixty miles inside the border. Wavell's desert force, although outnumbered, began to drive them back on 9 December. The 6th Australian Division captured Benghazi on 6 February 1941 and the Allies controlled Cyrenaica. During the month he launched a series of offensives against the Italians in East Africa which led to the surrender of Addis Abbaba by the Italians on 6 April. Wavell had to reinforce Greece when it was invaded, leaving only one infantry and one armoured division to protect Cyrenaica. The German 5th Light Division, the first part of what was to become the Afrika Korps, started to arrive in Libya on 14 February 1941. The second division of the Afrika Korps to arrive in Libya was the 15th Panzer Division in mid-April 1941, under the command of Feldmarschall Erwin Rommel, who was later to become known as the Desert Fox. This brilliant general outmanoeuvred Wavell's ill-equipped force, a risk Wavell had perceived, and the Axis forces reached the Egyptian border on 11 April 1941. Thus the capture of Benghazi was to be the only Allied victory until the Battle of El Alamein on 23 October 1942. On the night of 23/24 October the attack opened with a barrage from 1,000 guns. During a week of bitter fighting, losses mounted until Montgomery decided to make his major push on 2 November at Kidney Ridge. In the ensuing tank battles the Germans were decisively defeated and on 5 November, Rommel ordered a full retreat. This gave rise to the final surrender on 13 May 1943 of all the Axis forces in Africa.

The Star was gained by the service of one day in an operational area. The prerequisite of the 1939-1945 Star (GB.D017) was *not* necessary for the bestowal of this star. One of the three clasps could be added to the ribbon. These, however, differ from the others by virtue of the fact that they denote units as opposed to the award of another star and are self explanatory.

The ribbon comprises a sand-coloured 32 mm band, with a 9 mm central red stripe and a 2 mm dark blue stripe and a 2 mm light blue stripe on either side, flanking it by 5 mm. The colours represent the sand, red for the Army, dark blue the Navy and the light blue the Air Force.

GB.C004 North Africa 1942-1943 Clasp (naval and RAF personnel) GB.C005 Eighth Army Clasp (Army personnel) GB.C006 First Army Clasp (Army personnel)

There is no bronze clasp for these three awards; instead a silver rose is applied to the ribbon for GB.C004, a silver number '8' for GB.C005 and a silver number '1' for GB.C006. 18th

Army Group personnel who did not qualify for GB.C005 or GB.C006 were granted a silver rosette.

Right *The North Africa 1942-1943 Clasp (GB.C004)* (Spink & Son Ltd)

Above *Eighth Army Clasp (GB.C005)* (Spink & Son Ltd)

Above *First Army Clasp (GB.C006)* (Spink & Son Ltd)

GB.D021 Pacific Star

This Star will only be briefly described as it is outside the general scope of the coverage of this work. As with the previous stars (with the exception of GB.D020), the 1939-1945 Star (GB.D017) was a prerequisite for the award. The qualifying period was between the dates of 8 December 1941 and 2 September 1945. The recipient had to be engaged in operational service in the Pacific theatre. As with the other stars, winning one precluded the award of a second until a clasp had

been awarded.

The ribbon comprises a 32 mm band with 5.5 mm red edge stripes. These are flanked on the left by a 2.5 mm light blue stripe and on the right by a 2.5 mm dark blue one. The central panel is forest green with a central 3 mm yellow stripe. The colours emblematically represent green for the jungle, yellow for the Pacific beaches, red for the Army, dark blue for the Navy and light blue for the Air Force.

GB.C007 Pacific Clasp

As GB.C002.

Right *Pacific Clasp (GB.C007)* (Spink & Son Ltd)

GB.D022 Burma Star

This Star is also outside the main scope of this work and will thus be only covered briefly. It was to reward those troops who had been involved between 11 December 1941 and 2 September 1945 in the Burma campaign. Certain areas in the Bengal Province also qualified for the rendition of the award, which devalued it in the eyes of the recipients who had earned the Star in the steaming jungles of Burma with the 14th Army and its famous units such as the Chindits, commanded by the audacious and unconventional Orde Wingate. Those who subsequently received the award of the Pacific Star (GB.D021) received a clasp.

The ribbon comprises a 32 mm band with edge stripes of 5 mm dark blue, flanked by 5 mm orange and 5 mm dark blue. A central red panel of 9 mm is flanked by three stripes of the same configuration and colours.

GB.C008 Burma Clasp

As GB.C002.

Right *Burma Clasp (GB.C008)* (Spink & Son Ltd)

GB.D023 Italy Star

There was no prior time qualification for this Star, its qualifying time being from 11 June 1943 to 8 May 1945.

The Star could also be awarded for services rendered in the Aegean, Dodecanese, Corsica, Greece, Sardinia, Yugoslavia and Elba, while entry into Austria during the closing stages of the war even counted for the award. However, members of the Navy and the merchant navy had to have first received the 1939-1945 Star (GB.D017). There was no clasp authorized for either wear on this Star or to represent the Star on another ribbon.

The ribbon comprises a 32 mm band made up of the national colours of Italy in five equal stripes of red, white, green, white and red.

GB.D024 France and Germany Star

This Star was to reward service in France, Belgium, Holland and Germany. The prerequisite of having been awarded the 1939-1945 Star (GB.D017) was *not* necessary to the rendering of this star, only service between the qualifying dates of D-Day, and VE Day, 6 June 1944 to 8 May 1945 being necessary. The main intention of this Star was to reward some of the heaviest fighting of the whole war and as with the other stars (except GB.D023), the first gained precluded the award of a similar star.

The ribbon is a 32 mm band made up of five equal stripes of blue, white, red, white and blue, the three colours being the national colours of Britain, France and Holland. Belgium, it seems, was excluded in remembrance in the emblematical use of the colours in this ribbon.

GB.C009 France and Germany Clasp

As GB.C002.

Right *France and Germany Clasp (GB.C009)* (Spink & Son Ltd)

GB.D025 The Defence Medal

This Medal was to reward those members of auxiliary services, such as the fire service, air raid precautions, police and ambulance services as well as military personnel. The qualifying period for the Medal was between the dates of 3 September 1939 and 2 September 1945. There was no pre-requirement for the award of the 1939-1945 Star (GB.D017) and, in fact, The Defence Medal was harder to qualify for than some of the stars. It was necessary to have served for three years in the United Kingdom or six months overseas in territory subject to air attack. Service terminated by death or wounds due to enemy action was considered to render a person eligible. Those who had received a personal award conferred by the king were also eligible, irrespective of their length of service, provided they were serving in either category aforementioned. However, if a man or woman serving in the civil defence gained either the George Cross (GB.D002) or the George Medal (GB.D003), the recipient automatically became eligible for The Defence Medal, irrespective of category or service.

The obverse consists of the coinage type head of George VI with, in small raised capital letters beneath the truncation of the head, the initials of the designer, 'HP' for T. Hugh Paget. Round the edge of the medal is the circumscription 'GEORGIVS VI D:G: BR:OMN:REX: F:D: IND: IMP'.

The reverse design comprises a small stylized oak tree set on to a slightly convex ground surmounting two lines of waves running from left to right. On either side of the oak tree are two rampant lions facing one another but with their heads looking in opposite directions and upwards in roaring stance. Right paws are in a position to guard the tree, while the left ones are extended guarding against air attack. Surmounting the tree is a crown and in the roots is the designer's monogram, 'HWP', for Wilson Parker. The lower part of the medal has the inscription in two lines, 'THE   DEFENCE,   MEDAL', beneath which, on the lions' backs, at the medal's edge, are the dates 1939 and 1945. From the top of the medal there is a ball and straight bar suspender.

There are two versions of the medal: the first was issued to British Forces unnamed and produced in cupro-nickel; the second, Canadian, version was issued named and produced in silver, in a grade of .800 fine.

The ribbon comprises a 32 mm band of green, with a central orange-red stripe 8 mm wide, with two black stripes 1.5 mm wide on either side, inset from the edge by 4 mm. The green emblematically represents the green grass of England, the red the fires caused by the bombing and the black, the blackout.

GB.C010 Silver Laurel Leaves Clasp

There were no bars issued with The Defence Medal, (GB.D025) but there was one emblem of Silver Laurel Leaves authorized for wear on the ribbon. This was to denote the award of the King's Commendation for brave conduct. In 1943 a small plastic badge was worn on the left lapel of civilian clothing, while on the uniform of the merchant navy, civil defence, police and national fire service, it should be worn above the centre of the medal ribbon bar. This

was discontinued and replaced by the laurel emblem, which was applied to the ribbon.

GB.D026 The War Medal

This Medal was to reward military service during the Second World War. The qualifying period was the same as that for The Defence Medal (GB.D025) but it was only necessary to serve for 28 days in any of the armed forces, to gain entitlement. In the case of the merchant navy, the requirement was that the 28 days had to be served at sea. Provision was made for operational service terminated by death, wounds, disability or capture. In such cases, if the person had previously qualified for one of the campaign stars, the recipient was also entitled to the War Medal.

The obverse design comprises a crowned effigy of George VI with, at the truncation in small, raised capitals, the initials 'PM' of Percy Metcalfe the designer. The medal has the circumscription 'GEORGIVS VI D: G: BR: OMN: REX ET INDIAE IMP:'.

The reverse design is most striking in its subject matter, being a dragon with two heads. The heads have beaks. Standing on the back of this crouching or fallen dragon is a lion facing to the right, with three paws on the creature's carcase and the front offside on its head. Just above this head, in small raised capitals are the initials of the designer, 'E CRP' for E. Carter Preston. In two lines at the top of the medal, and to the left of the ball

of the suspender, are the dates 1939 over 1945. The suspender is of the straight bar variety.

Three types of the Medal can be encountered: first, the British forces award type which was produced in cupro-nickel and was issued unnamed; second, the Australian and South African award types which were also produced in cupro-nickel but awarded named; and third, the

Below Reverse The War Medal (GB.D026)

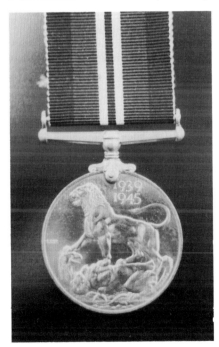

Canadian award type which was produced in silver .800 fine. It was awarded named to approximately 700,000 eligible Canadians. When rendered to the next of kin as well as the Canadian Memorial Cross (CM.D002) a silver Bar was added with the name and date of death attached to the ribbon.

No bars were awarded with this Medal but there was provision for the wearing of the Mentioned in Despatches device (GB.D027) on the ribbon. The ribbon comprised a 32 mm band that had five nearly equal stripes of red, blue, white, blue, red. The central white stripe contained an inner central stripe of red 2 mm wide.

GB.D027 Oak Leaf device for Mention in Despatches

King George VI authorized the wearing of a single oak leaf to recognize those Mentioned in Despatches during the Second World War. This practice had been introduced by George V, his father, in 1920 to acknowledge those who had earned them in the First World War. From its instigation in 1943, it was worn on the uniform jacket where medals would normally be found, and with the institution of The War Medal (GB.D026), it was applied to its ribbon. One emblem only was authorized to be worn so it is impossible to visually tell the number of mentions the recipient had been awarded.

Awards to civilian organizations

This chapter covers the Territorial Army Volunteer Units whose importance cannot be underestimated. The Special Constabulary took on a very important role in releasing valuable manpower from the regular police force to be used in all three Services' policing activities. Something often overlooked by military commentators is the importance of an active policing of the military services and the resources that these duties, in fact, take up. The rapid growth of the military also facilitated a comparable growth in crimes committed by those personnel. The importance of protecting military installations in the UK against bombing, by anti-aircraft fire and radar, as well as defending against invasion by the feared parachutists, to both of which the Territorial Army stationed in Great Britain attended, is also often underestimated.

Below *John W. Ailsby leads the Isle of Ely contingent of the Civil Defence at the victory parade held at Whittlesey to mark the end of the Second World War. His second in command, Dr James Popplewell to his immediate right, salutes the War Memorial in recognition of those who fell in the two World Wars.*

Index to civilian Awards

GB.D028 Territorial Efficiency Medal — 1930

This Medal was introduced in 1930 and replaced a number of other decorations that rewarded service with the volunteer units. However, I will not go into the history of these or their varying types as they are outside the scope of this book.

The design of the Medal comprises an oval which has a raised edge rim. On to the flat field is placed a crowned effigy of George VI, the effigy being complete with an ornate collar and a cross or decoration at the neck. The circumscription on it is 'GEORGIVS VI. D.G.BR OMN. REX.ET.INDIAE.IMP.', the 'A' and 'E' of 'Indiae' being formed in a diphthong. Beneath the truncation appear the designer's initials 'PM' in small raised capitals, which stood for Percy Metcalfe.

The reverse is plain, with a three-line inscription, 'FOR, EFFICIENT, SERVICE', in large raised capitals. The finish of the reverse surface is matt, while that of the obverse is mirror polished. From the top of the medal is an ornate ball suspender, with a spray of stylized leaves in the form of a 'V', with a scroll across containing the word 'TERRITOR-IAL' in raised capitals.

The Medal was issued named, with the recipient's name and initials, rank, service number and unit. An interesting point to note is that other decoration abbreviations were also added to the end of the inscription, e.g. 'MM' for Military Medal (GB.D010) after the name.

Below *Obverse The Territorial Efficiency Medal (GB.D028)*

The Medal was awarded to officers and other ranks of the Territorial Army who were serving on the active list of that force on 2 September 1939 and who had completed twelve years' service. A Bar is worn on the ribbon after the completion of eighteen years' service, with a further Bar to represent completion of 24 years' service. However, war service counted as double service time, thus any territorial soldier who joined in September 1939 became eligible for the medal by the completion of the war. Officers who already possessed the Efficiency Decoration (GB.D029), were disbarred from receiving an award of the Medal. However, if a man was in possession of the Medal plus the eighteen year Bar he could, after twenty years' service, be awarded the Efficiency Decoration (GB.D029).

The ribbon comprises a 32 mm green band, with 5 mm yellow edge stripes.

GB.D029 Efficiency Decoration — 1930

This Decoration, like the previous one, replaced a number of earlier volunteer decorations. The condi-

Below *Obverse The Efficiency Decoration (GB.D029)* (Spink & Son Ltd)

tions for its award in respect of service rendered during the Second World War were laid down in 1940. The insignia comprises an oval wreath of oak leaves, the leaves pointing downwards with cross ties at 3, 6, 9 and 12 o'clock respectively. The centre of the insignia has the royal monogram of George VI, surmounted by a crown. The wreath measures 39 mm by 32 mm and is coloured silver, with the ties, royal cypher and crown being finished in gilt. The top of the insignia has an eyelet through which passes the ribbon ring and, at the top of the ribbon is a bar with, in capital letters, 'TERRITORIAL ARMY'. Thus the ribbon runs from the bar to the ribbon ring.

The purpose of the Decoration was to reward efficient and capable officers who had served for twenty years and, as in the case of GB.D028, war service counted as double time.

The ribbon comprises a 38 mm green band with a central yellow stripe measuring 9 mm. Another ribbon that can be found on the Decoration comprises a 38 mm band, red on the right-hand side and blue on the left, with 3 mm yellow edge stripes. This ribbon is used by officers of the

Honourable Artillery Company, who have gained permission from the Colonel Commandant after having fulfilled certain qualifications of service. This privilege is not automatic but is still in practice today.

GB.D030 Special Constabulary Long Service Medal — August 1918

This Medal was introduced by George V in August 1918 to commemorate war service completed during the First World War. The Medal was continued and amended in 1940, the description following being relevant to the Second World War. The obverse design comprises a bareheaded effigy of George VI, known as the coinage type, with the inscription, 'GEORGIVS VI D:G:BR: OM N:REX F:D:IND:IMP'. Beneath the truncation of the head are two small raised initials in capitals, 'HP', these being for the designer, T. Hugh Paget.

The reverse comprises a pair of laurel sprays which have a tie at their base. The left spray runs round the edge of the medal, while that on the right runs across the bottom. The inscription in six lines fills the field, with the last line running over the top of the right spray of the laurel wreath and superimposing the left. The inscription is 'FOR, FAITHFUL, SERVICE, IN THE, SPECIAL, CONSTABULARY'. The top of the medal has a ball and claw, straight bar suspender. The Medal was issued named with the recipient's name and initials in impressed capitals.

To qualify for war service, a Special Constable must have served without pay for not less than three years and during that period have performed a minimum of fifty police duties, and to have been recommended by a chief officer of police as a member who was willing and competent to discharge the duties of a Special Constable.

The ribbon comprises a 32 mm white band, with a central 12 mm red stripe with 4 mm black edge stripes inset by 2 mm.

Below *Obverse Special Constabulary Long Service Medal George VI First type (GB.D030)* (Simon Norris)

Awards to Commonwealth troops by their respective countries

This chapter is broken down into the individual countries and the awards and flying wings of those countries, discussed in the relevant sub-chapters. Flying insignia which, basically, were much the same as those employed by the RAF, are covered in the relevant sections.

Changes in the design are usually only in the pilots' wings, generally in the central boss which is changed to the initials of the relevant flying service of each individual country, whereas the aircrew wings are of the same basic design as those employed in the RAF.

Below *Squadron Leader Fox, third on the left, is one of this cheerful bunch of Number 83 Squadron posing for the Press at Scampton, circa February 1941. He went on to be involved with volunteers from many Commonwealth countries.*

Index to Commonwealth Awards

Above *Reverse The Territorial Efficiency Medal (GB.D028)*

Above right *Reverse Special Constabulary Long Service Medal George VI First type (GB.D030)* (Simon Norris)

Right *Obverse Canadian Memorial Cross George VI type (CM.D002)* (James Cross. Collection Albert Flipts)

Above left *Reverse The South Africa Service Medal (CM.D003)* (Spink & Son Ltd)

Above *Reverse The Australian Service Medal (CM.D004)* (Spink & Son Ltd)

Left *Reverse The New Zealand War Service Medal (CM.D005)* (Spink & Son Ltd)

Above *Reverse The King's Medal for Courage in the Cause of Freedom [Courage] (GB.D031)* (Spink & Son Ltd)

Right *Legion of Honour – Grand Cross and Star (FR.D001)*

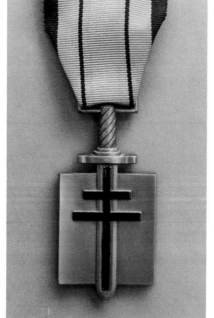

Above left *Reverse Legion of Honour –
Chevalier or Knights' Cross (FR.D007) with
variation of ribbon suspension* (Spink & Son
Ltd)

Above *Obverse Order of the Liberation
(FR.D008) with First pattern ribbon* (Josef
Charita)

Left *Obverse Order of the Liberation
(FR.D008)* (Josef Charita)

Above *a mixed group of young flyers from the Commonwealth, wearing a variety of insignia. The Sergeant at the bottom right wears the Canada patch and Air Gunners' Wing (CM.A004). The pilot at the centre is newly qualified and wears the Australian Pilots' Wings. He was killed in a plane crash, resulting from enemy ack-ack sustained over Germany, at Eastrea Whittlesey on his return from his first operational bombing mission, when he made up an eight-man crew of a Lancaster.*

CM.D001 Canadian Volunteers Service Medal 1939-1947 — 1943

This Medal was introduced in 1943 to reward those Canadians who had volunteered for service during the Second World War. It is a circular medal produced in silver with a raised edge rim. On the obverse, inset from the rim by approximately 2 mm, is the inscription '1939 CANADA 1945' running clockwise from 2 o'clock to 10 o'clock at the top. The lower portion of the medal has the inscription, running counter-clockwise,

'VOLUNTARY SERVICE VOLONTAIRE', the word 'SERVICE' being flanked on either side by a small maple leaf. This reflects Canada's dual language heritage.

Within the flat field of the medal so encompassed is the central design of seven marching figures, three men and three women to represent the three armed forces, followed up in the rear by a nurse. The men are placed in the foreground and the

Above *Obverse Canadian Volunteer Service Medal 1939-1947 (CM.D001) with Bar* (Spink & Son Ltd)

women in the background. The obverse was designed by the Canadian Army war artist, Major C.F. Comfort. Attached to the top edge of the medal is a round eyelet, through which passes a ring which passes through another eyelet in the bottom of the suspender. The suspender has two small projections from beneath its main line, which is chamfered with a mitred corner at each end and a raised chamfer. There are two rolled balls at the top, one at each end,

through which are placed a bar for the ribbon to pass through. The reverse of the medal bears the Canadian coat of arms. It was decided that the medal should be issued unnamed.

A Bar was authorized to be worn on the ribbon and comprises an oblong box with, inset by approximately 2 mm, a raised panel with chamfered edges. In the centre of this is placed a maple leaf emblem. Approximately a million Bars were issued.

The period of time required for eligibility was a minimum of eighteen months' honourable service, the qualifying period being calculated from 2 September 1939 to 1 March 1947. It was awarded to all ranks who had served honourably for the period. However, the Medal was awarded posthumously to any member of the forces who had been killed in action, or had died of wounds sustained in action or in the line of duty. The time limit was waived for such men and women, as well as those who had served outside Canada or been honourably discharged or retired. The Bar was awarded for services abroad.

The ribbon comprises a 38 mm blue band, with 6 mm green edge stripes, bordered by a 4 mm red stripe on either side.

CM.D002 Canadian Memorial Cross — 27 August 1940

This Cross was originally introduced on 1 December 1919 and was reintroduced for the Second World War

on 27 August 1940 to commemorate those who died in service. It consists of a small silver cross, not unlike the

British Military Cross (GB.D009). The arms of the cross are of equal length and straight, with a slight concave curve to the ends. Round the edges of the arms is a slight ridge and the field is raised. On to this is superimposed another matching cross, but in this case there is no curve at the ends. The arms of the cross have 'V's inset in their ends and there is a raised central spine. At the cross's centre is King George VI's cypher and on the upper arm, the imperial crown, while each of the other three 'V's has a maple leaf. The angles of the arms of the cross have a laurel leaf wreath, comprising three leaves which overlap in each bunch and two bunches of leaves to each quadrant. The gap between the wreath and the cross is segmented. From the upper arm above the crown, is an eyelet through which is a silver split ring with a piece of ribbon running through it. The cross measures 32 mm by 32 mm and is patinated.

The reverse is plain and flat, with the name, rank and serial number of the deceased. On the lower arm is positioned, in small capitals, the hall-mark and 'STERLING'. The medal was awarded in a small black box with an artificial pebbled leather finish, with chamfered edges and the impe-rial crown stencilled in silver in the middle of the upper lid. The inside has a white silk lid liner and white felt base which is hinged and can be lifted up, so allowing the ribbon to be put underneath, so that it holds the Cross in place as there is no recess in which the Cross can fit.

The Cross was to honour those who had died in the service of the country including Army, Navy, Air Force, Canadian merchant seamen and members of the Corps of Civilian Fire Fighters. The Cross was awarded to mothers and widows of the deceased and in the eventuality of there being both, two Crosses were awarded. The women then wore the cross in memoriam. It was worn on a violet ribbon of either 10-11 mm or approximately 27 mm wide. (Another interesting point, the widow of Squadron Leader Fox informed me that when she visited ex-members of 103 Squadron in Cana-da, she found that the widows also wore the decorations of the deceased round their necks on a silver chain. She thus had eyelets attached to the Distinguished Flying Medal (GB.D015) to facilitate its wear on formal occasions.)

Below *Reverse Canadian Memorial Cross George VI type (CM.D002)* (James Cross. Collection Albert Flipts)

CM.A001 RCAF Pilots' Wings

The Pilots' Wings are identical to those employed by the RAF (GB.A001), save for the change in the monogram which consists of the cypher 'R.A.F.' surmounting a large 'C' positioned in the wreath. The emblem was worn above the left breast pocket, above any ribbons or decorations.

Above *RCAF Pilots' Wings (CM.A001)*

CM.A002 RCAF Navigators' Wing

This is identical to the RAF counterpart (GB.A006), save that instead of the wreath bow the initials in capitals, 'R.C.A.F.' appear, and the apex of the wreath has a king's crown with a red underlay to its arches. The emblem was worn above the left breast pocket, above any ribbons or decorations.

Left *RCAF Navigators' Wing (CM.A002)*

CM.A003 RCAF Bomb Aimers' Wing

This is identical to the RAF counterpart (GB.A008) apart from the same differences as in CM.A002.

Right *RCAF Bomb Aimers' Wing (CM.A003)*

CM.A004 RCAF Air Gunners' Wing

As CM.A003 (GB.A003).

Left *RCAF Air Gunners' Wing (CM.A004)*

CM.A005 RCAF Wireless Operator Air Gunners' Wing

As CM.A003 (GB.A010).

Right *RCAF Wireless Operator Air Gunners' Wing (CM.A005)*

CM.A006 RCAF Flight Engineers' Wing

As CM.A003 (GB.A004).

Left *RCAF Flight Engineers' Wing (CM.A006)*

CM.D003 The South African Service Medal 1939-1945 — 16 November 1943

Above *Obverse The South Africa Service Medal (CM.D003)* (Spink & Son Ltd)

This design comprises a round medal with a raised edge. The obverse has a circumscription, 'AFRICA SERVICE MEDAL', on the right side and 'AFRIKADIENS — MEDALJA' on the left, illustrating the dual languages of the country, English and Afrikaans. On the central field is a contoured map of Africa.

The reverse shows a scene of the African Velt on to which is superimposed a Springbok leaping to the right.

From the top is a claw suspender with straight arms. The medal was produced in silver and officially named in indented block capitals with a prefix, either 'N' for a native recipient or 'C' for a coloured.

The Medal was issued to all full-time service members of the Union of South Africa's fighting forces who had served either at home or abroad and had completed thirty days' service in South Africa and who had attested for service before 13 May 1943, this being the date on which the enemy had finally been cleared from Africa. It is estimated that 192,000 awards of this Medal were bestowed.

The ribbon comprises a 32 mm band, with an orange centre and 3 mm outer green and 3 mm inner yellow edges. A bronze protea leaf is worn on the ribbon to denote either a Mention in Despatches (GB.D027) or a King's Commendation (GB. C010).

South African Air Force Wings
CM.A007 SAAF Pilots' Wings

This badge employs a pair of wings similar to those used by the RAF to

denote pilots (GB.A001), but with at the centre a white instead of a bronze

Above *SAAF Pilots' Wings (CM.A007)*

wreath, running around a shield. The shield is quartered and comprises two yellow panels situated diagonally opposite one another, the other two being red and green. On these are placed the figure of Hope to repres-ent the Cape Province, the Wildebeest of Natal, the Orange Tree of the Orange Free State and the Oxcart or wagon for the Transvaal. This shield is surmounted by a king's crown with red insets in the arches.

The emblem was worn above the left breast pocket, above any ribbons or decorations.

CM.D004 The Australian Service Medal 1939-1945 — 1 December 1949

J.B. Chipley, the Prime Minister of Australia introduced this Medal on 1 December 1949. It was produced from cupro-nickel and has, as its obverse design, the crowned head of George VI with the inscription, 'GEORGIVS VI D:G:BR:OM N: REX ET INDIAE IMP:'. The reverse has the circumscription, 'THE AUS-TRALIAN SERVICE MEDAL', with the dates 1939-1945 at the base, with a gap between the beginning and the end of the legend. The central field contains the coat of arms of Australia. The top of the medal has a ball and claw straight bar suspender. The edge rim has the recipient's name and initials with the regimental or service number impressed in capitals.

This Medal was to reward all the Australians in the armed forces, as well as the Australian Mercantile Marine, who had between 3 September 1939 and 2 September 1945, served for a minimum of eighteen months overseas. However, honoura-ble discharge, retirement or service (whether full or part time) termi-nated by death, wounds or any disability also qualified the recipient.

It is estimated that 177,000 were issued.

The ribbon comprises a 32 mm band, with a 14 mm khaki centre flanked by 1.5 mm red stripes, the edges being dark blue on the viewer's left and pale blue on the right. These colours emblematically represent dark blue for the Navy, khaki for the Army, light blue the Air Force, and red for the mercantile marines.

Royal Australian Air Force Wings
CM.A008 RAAF Pilots' Wings

This badge comprises a pair of wings of the same design as those employed by the RAF (GB.A001), but in this case, the wreath is finished in blue as opposed to bronze. The RAF cypher is replaced by the monogram 'R.A.A.F.' which is placed in the centre of the wreath. These were worn above the left breast pocket, above any ribbons or decorations.

CM.A009 RAAF Observers' Wing

The insignia is the same basic design as used by the RAF (GB.A002), but the wreath is finished in blue and the underlay is also of airforce blue. The emblem was worn above the left breast pocket, above any ribbons or decorations.

CM.A010 RAAF Air Gunners' Wing

As CM.A009 (GB.A003).

CM.A011 RAAF Bomb Aimers' Wing

As CM.A009 (GB.A008).

CM.A012 RAAF Signallers' Wing

As CM.A009 (GB.A009).

CM.D005 The New Zealand War Service Medal 1939-1945

The Medal comprises, on the obverse, the bare head of George VI that was employed in the design of the coinage of Great Britain. It has the inscription, 'GEORGIVS VI D:G: BR: OM N:' (the claw of the suspender obliterating the 'O') 'REX F:D: IND: IMP.', with the initials 'HP' in small raised capitals beneath the truncation of the head, these being those of the designer and engraver, T. Hugh Paget.

The reverse has a raised edge and a flat field, on to which is placed in four lines, the inscription and date, 'FOR, SERVICE TO, NEW ZEALAND, 1939 1945', surmounting a fern frond, pointing to the viewer's right.

The suspender is attached by a ball with two fern fronds finished on either side, formed in a 'V', with upturned ends through which is placed the bar for the ribbon to run under. The medal was constructed of cupro-nickel and was issued unnamed, approximately 238,000 being produced. (Whether this is the issued number or just the production run delivered to the New Zealand government is unknown to this author.)

The Medal was to reward all those members of the New Zealand fighting forces who had served at home or abroad between the dates of 3 September 1939 and 2 September 1945 and who, between those dates, had completed at least 28 days' full-time service. However, honourable discharge, retirement or when ser-

Below *Obverse The New Zealand War Service Medal (CM.D005)* (Spink & Son Ltd)

vice, whether full or part time, was terminated by death, wounds or any disability, qualified the recipient for the bestowal of the award. This is similar to the other Commonwealth awards, with one other proviso: if the service was terminated by capture by the enemy, the recipient must be free from blame for being captured.

The ribbon comprises a 32 mm black watered ribbon with white edges that measure 4.5 mm.

Royal New Zealand Air Force Wings
CM.A013 RNZAF Pilots' Wings

This badge comprises a pair of wings of the same design as that employed by the RAF (GB.A001), with a similar wreath of the same colour but with the monogram 'NZ' replacing the RAF cypher. These were worn above the left breast pocket, above any ribbons or decorations.

Above *RNZAF Pilots' Wings (CM.A013)*

CM.A014 RNZAF Pilots' Wings Alternative Pattern

This badge comprises a pair of wings of the same design as that employed by the RAF (GB.A001) with a similar wreath of the same colour but with the monogram 'RNZAF' replacing the RAF cypher. These were worn above the left breast pocket, above any ribbons or decorations.

CM.A015 RNZAF Air Gunners' Wing

The insignia is the same basic design as used by the RAF (GB.A003), but with the addition of the crown above the letter, as in the wing (CM.A002) and the substitution of the letters RNZAF. It was worn above the left breast pocket, above any ribbons or decorations.

CM.A016 RNZAF Bomb Aimers' Wing

As CM.A015 (GB.A008).

CM.A017 RNZAF Signallers' Wing

As CM.A015 (GB.A009).

CM.A018 RNZAF Navigators' Wing

As CM.A015 (GB.A006).

Right *RNZAF Navigators' Wing (CM.A018)*

CM.A019 RNZAF Wireless Operator Air Gunners' Wing

As CM.A015 (GB.A010).

CM.A020 RNZAF Flight Engineers' Wing

As CM.A015 (GB.A007).

Medals awarded to foreign subjects by the British government

The medals that had been awarded to foreign subjects in the First World War, who had substantially helped the British cause or personnel in either occupied Europe or Germany herself, were reintroduced. The help that was given to Allied airmen in the Second World War was of immense assistance to the war effort. The financial cost, as well as the time to train aircrew and pilots, was considerable and the varying Resistance escape routes enabled 2,803 airmen to evade capture in Europe alone, resulting in them being brought to safety. In 1945 more than 14,000 helpers were identified as having given significant assistance in these matters. The cost of this assistance and help was often severe, for those caught usually faced execution by firing squad or imprisonment in concentration camps where many suffered grievously.

Index to medals awarded to foreign subjects

GB.D031 The King's Medal for Courage in the Cause of Freedom 1947 (Courage) — 23 August 1945

The Medal is constructed of silver and has, as its obverse design, the crowned head of George VI with the title, 'GEORGIVS VI D:G:BR:

Above *Obverse The King's Medal for Courage in the Cause of Freedom [Courage] (GB.D031* (Spink & Son Ltd)

OMN: REX ET INDIAE IMP:'. Beneath the truncation of the head are the initials, in small raised capitals, 'PM', which stood for the designer and engraver Percy Metcalfe, while the reverse design was executed by W.M. Gardner (even though the Royal Mint annual report attributed the design to T.H. Paget).

The reverse design consists of a chain that runs round the edge, inset by approximately 2 mm and comprising 39 links. On the flat field is placed the inscription in five lines, 'THE KINGS, MEDAL FOR, COURAGE, IN THE CAUSE OF, FREEDOM'. The upper and lower two lines are the same relative height while 'COURAGE' is in larger letters. At the base, approximately 1 mm above the chain, are the designer's initials, in small raised capitals, 'WG'. From the top of the medal is a ball suspender raised on a plinth. Through the ball is a round ribbon ring.

The first issues of the Medal were made in 1947 and a total of approximately 3,200 were finally awarded, all of which were presented unnamed. The Medal was to reward Allied civilians or other foreigners who had risked torture and death while undertaking dangerous assignments, such as those encountered in the prosecution of resistance work, where exceptional courage had been shown; or in the organization or operation of escape lines that enabled British and Commonwealth personnel to avoid capture.

The ribbon comprises a 32 mm white band with 6 mm red edges and two 2.5 mm central blue stripes, spaced 1.5 mm apart.

GB.D032 The Kings' Medal for Courage in the Cause of Freedom 1947 (Service) — 23 August 1945

This silver medal has, as its obverse design, the crowned head of George VI with the title, 'GEORGIVS VI D:G:BR:OMN: REX ET INDIAE

Above *Reverse The King's Medal for Courage in the Cause of Freedom [Service] (GB.D032)* (Spink & Son Ltd)

IMP:'. Beneath the truncation of the head are the initials in small raised capitals, 'PM', for Percy Metcalfe. The reverse design was executed by T.H Paget and consisted of a circumscription, 'FOR SERVICE IN THE CAUSE OF FREEDOM'. The inscription starts and ends at a line

that produces a ground containing a knight in armour, without his helmet. This is placed on the ground, between his spread legs. He holds in his right hand a broken lance, which is placed butt to the ground and point resting on his right shoulder. He is facing to the left and is confronted by a young woman dressed in flowing mediaeval garb. She is facing to the right and is holding in her right hand a picture which she offers to the knight, emblematically to represent the gift of food and water. The field beneath the ground has, in two lines, the inscription 'THE KING'S, MEDAL'. From the top of the medal is a ball suspender raised on a plinth, through which is a round ribbon ring.

The first issues of the Medal were made in 1947 and a total of approximately 2,490 were finally awarded, all of which were presented unnamed. The Medal was to reward Allied civilians and foreigners for services that furthered the interests of Great Britain, her Commonwealth and allies. These services could range over a wide field and where the element of danger or death did not normally occur.

The ribbon comprises a 32 mm white band with three equally spaced stripes, red in the centre and blue at either side that measured 3 mm.

Awards of France and the Free French forces

France had lain like a slumbering giant. The eruption of the Second World War in September 1939 did little to change her posture. Her generals took defence behind the Maginot Line. This supposedly impregnable line of fortresses had been built to safeguard her like a chastity belt, from the ravages she had experienced during the First World War. When it had been completed in 1935, the cost had been a horrendous 7,000 million francs and the wall filled the gap between Switzerland and southern Belgium, with a line of independent fortified regions organized in three belts. On the frontier itself stood a line of pillboxes, entanglements and anti-tank obstacles. Behind that, lay a line of larger concrete casements and anti-tank ditches. Five miles to the rear of this, stood the forts which were spaced between three and five miles apart. These underground battleships, as they had been called, with their electric railways, sun lamp rooms and disappearing gun turrets, the largest of which housed a total of 1,200 men, were considered a military wonder. However, due to Belgian sensitivity, the line was curtailed at the tip of the Ardennes.

In the early dawn of 10 May 1940, after the period of the 'phoney war', Germany invaded the Low Countries while the French and British were engaging what they imagined to be the main thrust in the north. Hitler struck through the supposedly impregnable Ardennes and encircled the BEF, compelling it to evacuate by sea from Dunkirk. The Maginot Line was thus bypassed and was consequently never a factor in the Battle of France. German armour began to pour, virtually unopposed, into France. Paul Reynaud, who had taken over the Premiership from Daladier on 21 March, reshuffled his cabinet to allow for the inclusion of firstly de Gaulle and on 6 June to bring in Chantemps and Pétain as vice premiers. On 15 June the government moved to Bordeaux, Reynaud's intention being to set up government in North Africa to enable him to continue the war. A major rift had appeared in the government and two diametrically opposed political routes were emerging, that to become the Free French and that to become Vichy France. Truly a nation divided, a fact that was soon to become an ideological as well as a geographical reality. Reynaud, unable to command sufficient support, resigned on 17 June 1940 and President Lebrun called on Pétain to form a government. Pétain, within hours of taking office, made a radio broadcast to the nation in which he announced he had asked for an armistice. This was granted and was signed on 22 June, in the same railway carriage in the forest of Compiègne in which Foch had received the surrender of the Germans in 1918.

De Gaulle, who was one of the original dissenters to the armistice, made his way to England in an attempt to continue the fight. The structure of the French forces and the fighting that took place, the formations of the units which comprised the Free French Army, Air Force and Navy, the rivalry between the two opposing Free French high commands, that of General de Gaulle based in London and that of General Giraud based in North Africa, and the American interplay between the two commands, would fill a volume or volumes on their own. Suffice it to say that I have not included these breakdowns but tried to bring the political thought behind the medals to the reader. France, through Pétain, was the only country to sign an armistice with Hitler and this put her in a special international legal position, as it did those troops who fought either with the Allies, or the Germans. The position of the Germans in France was also different, as was that of its security police, witness the case of Claus Barbie and his relationship with the Resistance. However, this very involved position gave rise to the medals discussed in this chapter and the bravery of those who fought and suffered during the struggle for the liberation of La Belle France.

Index to Free French Awards

French Air Force Wings

French Naval Flying Badges

British awards to French nationals

	Medal	1st Bar	2nd Bar
GB.D005 Order of the British Empire — Gallantry	1		
GB.D006 The Distinguished Service Cross	35	3	1
GB.D008 The Conspicuous Gallantry Medal (R.N.)	1		
GB.D009 Military Cross	135		
GB.D010 Military Medal	185		
GB.D011 The Distinguished Conduct Medal	20		
GB.D012 The Distinguished Flying Cross	201	6	
GB.D013 The Air Force Cross	6		
GB.D015 The Distinguished Flying Medal	33		

Legion of Honour

On 19 May 1802, to replace the orders of the former royal family of France, which had been abolished since 30 July 1791, Napoleon Bonaparte perceived the necessity for a decoration to reward the courage of his troops. Consequently the decoration was brought into existence in four classes. 1805 brought about a review of the decoration and thenceforth there was an extension of the classes or grades, to five. However, in 1816, there was the final reorganization which basically was a fine tuning operation and these grades have been carried through to the present day. Thus, the decoration can be conferred upon French and

foreign recipients for military bravery as well as for civil achievement.

The order is controlled and governed by a Chancellor who is elected for life. The Chancellor receives recommendations from the relevant minister of the government or the Chancellor himself. He then communicates these recommendations or promotions within the order to the President of France for approval. The President holds the rank of Grand Master of the Legion, as part of his formal presidential duties and he then approves the promotions or the award of the order to the recipient.

In 1870 political pressures in France led to the fall of the second empire and with it, the last monarch of France, Napoleon III. This brought about the introduction of the legend, 'REPUBLIQUE FRANCAIS', and the date 1870. With the change in the legend came the abolition of the crown that had been used as the ribbon suspender and the introduction of an oval green laurel wreath in its stead. There is no design distinction indicating whether the decoration has been awarded for military or civil achievement but when rendered in wartime for gallantry in action, it is accompanied by the bestowal of the Croix de Guerre (FR.D010) Avec Palme. For regularity and to indicate the last change in the legend, although outside the scope of this work, a star replaced the 1870 date in 1951, which helps to identify a post-war piece from one that was produced before 1951.

FR.D001 Legion of Honour — Grand Cross Star — 1870

The Star is produced in silver and comprises a central boss or medallion. This is circular and has a raised outer line. There is a similar inner line producing a 'tramline'. The field produced between the two lines is minutely pebbled and frosted; on to this is the inscription 'REPUBLIQUE FRANCAIS 1870' and at the beginning and end a circle of pellets in a starlike pattern, five in number. Beaneath the pellets is a further inscription, 'HONNEUR ET PATRIE'. The whole of this inscription is polished, the height of the letters coming to the same relative height as that of the tramlines. The central field is polished and has, as its central motif, a classical head facing to the left, the viewer's right, that symbolizes the female Head of the Republic. This head is frosted. From this medallion emanate five arms of a cross that broaden at their extremity with a 'V' cut into their end. At each tip of the 'V' is a ball finial. The cross's arms are outlined with a raised edge, which is mirrored by a matching 'tramline'. These 'tramlines' are filled with diamond-shaped pellets, while the arms have their fields made up with diagonal diamond-shaped designs. Between the arms of the

Below *Legion of Honour - Grand Cross Star (FR.D001)* (Josef Charita)

cross are five pencil rays. Each of the rays is outlined with a line of hand raised pellets which are frosted, while the central panel, between these pellets, is thrown up and mirror polished.

The reverse is gently concave with a massive retaining pin.

FR.D002 Legion of Honour — Grand Cross Sash Badge — 1870

This badge consists, as does the Star, of a central boss or medallion with a raised edge line, and a parallel inner line but, in the case of this insignia, the field created in those 'tramlines' is enamelled in dark blue. On to this is applied the inscription 'REPUB-LIQUE FRANCAIS' and the date 1870.

The cross is constructed of five arms that radiate from the boss. The arms widen at the outer edge with a 'V' cut into each end. The points thus formed are surmounted by a ball finial. There is an outer edge line that acts as a border to the field produced which is filled with opaque white enamel. Between the arms of the cross runs a wreath of oak and laurel leaves, with a tie that drops vertically between the lower two arms directly beneath the date. The oak leaves make up the left-hand portion and are separated and enamelled green, while a similar laurel spray occupies the opposite side, once again enamelled green.

From the 'V' of the upper arm is a stirrup or box suspender, to which is placed the hinge which is attached to an oval wreath of oak and laurel leaves, in this case the composition of the wreath being in the opposite position to that on the cross. Also they are close together with no individual leaves, only the outline of the individual leaves that make up the inner and outer edges of the wreath. The hinge is formed by the bow tie at the base of the wreath, to which is attached an acorn on one side and a laurel berry on the other. There are a further two acorns and three laurel berries on the wreath. At the apex of the wreath is a ribbon cross and from this rises a decorative eyelet, to which is attached the ring that allows the insignia to be attached to the sash by its hook.

The reverse design has 'HON-NEUR ET PATRIE' on the border of the medallion or boss, with two crossed tricolors taking the central design of the medallion. The overall colour of both the obverse and reverse is gilt.

The sash is red and measures 102 mm. It is worn over the right shoulder and falls to the left hip where a bow is positioned. The bow ends have three layers, two of them being cut in a pinked design to produce a dogtooth edge.

FR.D003 Legion of Honour — Grand Officers' Star — 1870

This star is identical to the Grand Cross Star, FR.D001, and is worn in conjunction with the Officers' Cross, FR.D006, on the right breast of the recipient.

FR.D004 Legion of Honour — Grand Officers' Cross — 1870

This is identical to the Officers' Cross (FR.D006) and will be discussed at that point. It is also worn in a similar manner on a chest ribbon with a rosette and in conjunction with the Star (FR.D003) on the right breast of the recipient.

FR.D005 Legion of Honour — Commanders' Neck Cross — 1870

This is identical to the Sash Badge (FR.D002) but is worn at the throat of the recipient, the eyelet being converted to a suspender through which the neck ribbon is threaded.

FR.D006 Legion of Honour — Officers' Cross — 1870

This badge is of the same general design as the Grand Cross Sash Badge (FR.D002) but approximately only four-fifths the size. The cross' wreath is also less distinct because of the fact that, due to the size, the leaves were not so individually separated. The suspension wreath is also identical save for the fact that the ornate eyelet is replaced by a ball, through which passes the ribbon ring to which the ribbon is attached.

The reverse has 'HONNEUR ET PATRIE' on the blue border that fills the 'tramlines' and crossed tricolors on the central boss or medallion. The ribbon is red and measures 38 mm aproximately, on to which is attached a rosette. The whole Cross is worn on the right breast.

Left *Obverse Legion of Honour - Officers' Cross (FR.D006)* (Josef Charita)

FR.D007 Legion of Honour — Chevalier or Knights' Cross — 1870

This insignia is identical to the previous one save, in this case, all the metal parts of the cross are silver, with only the medallion or central boss being gilded. The ribbon is also red and approximately 38 mm in width. It does not have the addition of the rosette but is also worn on the right breast.

Right *Obverse Legion of Honour - Chevalier or Knights' Cross (FR.D007) with variation of ribbon suspension* (Spink & Son Ltd)

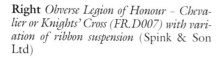

FR.D008 Order of the Liberation — 16 November 1940

General Charles de Gaulle had been brought into the French government as Under Secretary for War in May 1940. He was subsequently not prepared to support the French government's proposals for the opening of armistice negotiations with Germany and as a result of his refusal to concede defeat, escaped to London where, in June 1940, he declared the formation of 'Free French Forces'. His ambition was to annex Vichy territory to give validity to his claim of being the only independent legitimate French government and thus being able to negotiate with the

Below *Reverse Order of the Liberation (FR.D008)* (Josef Charita)

Allies the direction of the war. His claim to power was regarded somewhat sceptically by Britain and America, an attitude which led to a very uneasy relationship with de Gaulle which led him, in October 1940, to undertake an expedition in Dakar which ended in fiasco at best and a disaster at worst.

De Gaulle, the perceptive statesman, realized the need for an outward sign of recognition for the assistance afforded him by his French volunteers and other nationals, both military and civilian, who distinguished themselves in the furtherance of the liberation of France and the French empire during the Second World War. The Order of the Liberation was introduced on 16 November 1940 and discontinued on 23 January 1946; it was placed in order of preference behind the Legion of Honour and its recipients were honoured with the title of Compagnons de la Libération. This Order can be considered nearly as a personal award of General de Gaulle. He could also render the award upon a military unit as a unit citation.

The cross consists of an oblong shield on to which is placed, through the centre, a double-edged sword whose tip just breaks the bottom of the shield. The crossguard is just above the shield. The handle has a diagonal chequered grip with a stirrup suspender through the top. On to this, from the bottom of the crossguard to the tip of the handle, is placed the Cross of Lorraine. There are two variations of this basic design which are generally attributed to manufacturers' differences, or they could be a slight readjustment that coincided with the alteration in 1941 to the ribbon design which will be discussed later.

The first version has the space between the top of the shield and the bottom of the crossguard filled in and the Cross of Lorraine and the shield are in the same overall colour of patinated bronze. The second version has the gap between the shield and the bottom of the crossguard cut out and the Cross of Lorraine has an outline. The central field this produces is created in black, while the rest of the cross and shield is of patinated bronze.

The overall measurements of the rectangular plaque are 34 mm by 36 mm. The original manufacturer of

the insignia was John Pinches Ltd of London.

The reverse is plain, save for the inscription which is executed in large letters in four lines, 'PATRIAM, SERVANDO, VICTORIAM, TULIT', which translates as 'To serve the Fatherland brings Victory'.

The ribbon initially was an unwatered green, having narrow black diagonal stripes. In 1941 a revised ribbon was introduced that consisted of a watered green ribbon, 40 mm wide with black edges 4.5 mm wide and two black stripes, 15 mm apart, measuring 0.75 mm. The symbolism of the ribbon has been attributed to a representation of green which alludes to France's hope for the future and black to symbolize the death and mourning of the French people. As earlier stated, it is highly probable that it was at this time that the cross was also redesigned to incorporate the Black Cross of Lorraine.

FR.D009 The Médaille Militaire — 22 January 1852

The Medal was founded by Ludovic Napoleon Bonaparte who was the then President of France, on 22 January 1852 with the express purpose of being the country's highest military decoration. It is governed by the same Chancellor and Chancellery as that of the Legion of Honour. To underline the importance of the decoration and its interaction with the Legion of Honour, senior officers must first have received the bestowal of a class

of the Legion of Honour, to qualify for the award of this decoration. The Medal could also, in this case, be rendered posthumously to the recipient. It was thus decreed that the award was to be rendered to officers, NCOs and other ranks of the French forces and members of her Merchant Marine, who had distinguished themselves by heroic actions or who had received one or more wounds. It could be awarded for diplomatic reasons to allied military leaders and foreign civilians, or foreign nationals serving with or in the French armed forces. With these varying qualifications, it is estimated that the award has been rendered in excess of a million times since 1852.

There have been a number of designs of this medal but the one that is relevant to this work follows the design introduced in 1870, with the fall of the empire, and which incorporates the Head of the Republic facing to the right, surrounded by a raised line with another in parallel forming a 'tramline'. Between these two lines is a dark blue enamelled field with the inscription 'REPUBLIQUE FRANCAIS' and the date 1870 which is positioned below the truncation of the head, with a five-pointed star either side.

This central boss or medallion is surrounded by a laurel leaf wreath which has a crossed bow beneath the date. The edge of the medal follows the indentations of the wreath. At the top of the medal is a hinge concealed by a trophy of arms. This allows for the device to be attached to the medal and comprises a pair of crossed cannon barrels with an anchor that surmounts them, with one tip on each breech block. From the middle, where the cannons cross, is a breastplate or cuirass. From the top of the breastplate is a circle through which is placed the medal ribbon ring.

All the metal parts of the medal and the trophy of arms are gilded, including the wreath bow, while the wreath itself is silver. The reverse is the same in colour and the medallion inscription is 'VALEUR ET DISCIPLINE'.

The ribbon comprises a 38 mm yellow band with olive green edges that measure 5 mm in width.

FR.D010 Croix de Guerre 1939 — 26 September 1939

This Cross was introduced on 26 September 1939 to reward officers, NCOs and rank and file of the French forces as well as those of allied or friendly powers. French civilians were also entitled, as were foreign civilians and in exceptional circumstances, towns could receive the decoration. It could also be rendered as a unit citation to a military unit. The qualification for the award of the Cross was to have been Mentioned in Despatches.

The cross is constructed of bronze and measures 38 mm by 38 mm, this design being known as a cross pattée. The arms radiate from a central boss or medallion and widen at the ends. Round the arms is a raised edge which measures 2 mm and the field produced is lightly pebbled. The central boss is slightly convex and has a raised edge and another inset by 2 mm. Into this 'tramline' is the inscription 'REPUBLIQUE FRANCAIS' with, at the bottom, a star which has

Above left *Obverse Croix de Guerre (FR.D010), made in London* (Josef Charita)

Above right *Reverse Croix de Guerre (FR.D010) with Panel showing 1939* (Spink & Son Ltd)

Left *Obverse Croix de Guerre (FR.D010). This Cross was cast in North Africa.*

a branch either side with five leaves, one at the end and two on either side of the twig. The central field of the boss has the Head of the Republic facing to the left.

Through the angles of the arms of the cross are two crossed double-edged swords. From the top arm is a ball finial supported on a pair of scrolls which are back to back, and through this finial runs the ribbon ring. The reverse is identical save for the medallion, which has a solid line which measures 2 mm, and on the boss' field is found the date 1939. In some cases this has the addition of the date 1945 beneath it. There are several slight variations to this cross due to the quantity awarded and the number of different manufacturers.

The use of additional emblems of various types was continued from the previous 1914-1918 type and were attached to the ribbon. These were: the Bronze Palm and Bronze Laurel Branch, each representing an award for a Mention in Army Corps Despatches; Bronze Star for a Mention in Regiment or unit Despatches; Silver Star for a Mention in Brigade Despatches and Gilt Star for a Mention in Division Despatches.

The ribbon is green, 37 mm wide, with 8 mm red edges and three 1.5 mm red stripes in the centre of the ribbon placed 4 mm apart.

FR.D011 Croix de Guerre 1939-1940 — 28 March 1941

Although this cross was conceived by Marshal Philippe Pétain and thus is a Vichy French award and does not technically belong in this work, it would be incorrect not to include it because all those Frenchmen who received FR.D010 prior to the fall of France in 1940 had to return their orders for scrutiny, and did not have to have been supporters of the Vichy régime to have had the award. All those who had received the Croix de Guerre (FR.D010) under the Daladier and Reynaud governments, that is to say the Republican governments that were in power at the start of the war and at the time of the fall of France, had to return their decoration and after an examination of each individual case were issued with a new version of the award which was instituted on 28 March 1941. Apart from the fact that the reverse now has 1939-1940 in place of 1939, it is identical to the previous type.

The new ribbon design is green with black edge stripes and five black stripes measuring 1.5 mm. The addition of the insignia on the ribbon are the same as those found in the preceding description.

Below *Obverse Croix de Guerre 1939-1940 (FR.D011)*

FR.D012 Croix de Guerre 1943 — 1943

General Giraud instituted this award in 1943, to reward the troops under his command who were stationed in North Africa. He had it produced locally in North Africa, possibly Algeria, and the commissioning of this medal may have come about because of his rivalry with de Gaulle. Another view is that, owing to Giraud's isolation from de Gaulle and his government, this medal was conceived in this form by natural evolution due to the army's isolation. However, whatever the reason for this version, by an order of 7 January 1944 from the French National Committee of Liberation and General de Gaulle, it was discontinued and the Croix de Guerre FR.D010 was to be the only legitimate award for the Second World War. Thus the status of the three types was clarified and FR.D011 and FR.D012 both became obsolete because of their political disaffection from the Gaullist cause.

The design of the cross was identical to that of the Croix de Guerre 1939 (FR.D010) but in this case the obverse medallion has, as its design, crossed tricolors and on the reverse medallion the date 1943. The ribbon was also different, being that originally used for the Croix de Guerre 1914-1918, which was a green design 38 mm wide with thin red edge stripes and five red stripes 1.5 mm wide set 5 mm apart.

This Cross used the same emblems on the ribbon as were employed in FR.D010 to denote the various types of awards the recipient had received.

FR.D013 Croix de Guerre — Overseas Theatres of Operations — 26 September 1939

This Cross was reintroduced on 26 September 1939 and took the same design as the Croix de Guerre, with the same obverse medallion design. The reverse medallion had the inscription 'THÉÂTRES D'OPÉRATIONS EXTÉRIEURS'. The first and last words curve round the medal above and below the central one, which is ranged horizontally midway across the medallion. The ribbon comprises a 37 mm pale blue band, with a 9 mm red edge stripe.

FR.D014 Cross of Combatants — 28 June 1930

This Cross was introduced on 28 June 1930 for holders of the Combatants' Card. It consisted of a cross with straight arms that widen to the tips. Each arm has a raised edge line which runs two-thirds of the length of the arm. The obverse has a central medallion containing the Head of the Republic, while the reverse has a raised edge line, the field produced having a sword of the Roman type pointing downwards, with ten rays radiating from behind the hilt of the sword with the left and right ray horizontally positioned in line with the top of the crossguard of the sword. Beneath these rays runs the inscription 'CROIX DE. COMBATANTS'. The angles of the cross have a laurel leaf placed between them. This medal was extended to be used by veterans of the Second World War.

The ribbon comprises a green

Above *Obverse Cross of Combatants (FR.D014)* (Josef Charita)

band, 37 mm wide with an 8 mm red central stripe and side stripes inset by 1 mm of yellow, that measured 4 mm.

FR.D015 Cross of Combatants 1939-1940 — 28 March 1941

This Cross is again not an award of the Free French but that of the Vichy government. It comprises a cross of identical design to that of FR.D014 and on either side of the sword, in two lines, are the dates 1939, 1940.

The ribbon is sky blue with broad black edge stripes and three black central stripes, equally positioned and spaced from the edge stripes and one another.

FR.D016 Cross of Combatants Volunteers 1939-1945 — 4 February 1953

This Cross was instituted on 4 February 1953 and took the same basic design and purpose of the earlier Cross to reward the participants in the 1914-1918 war. It consists of a bronze patinated cross, the arms of which emanate from a central boss or medallion, on to which is the head of a soldier wearing a steel helmet and facing to the left. The arms of the cross measure 36 mm across and are similar to the Croix de Guerre (FR.D010), with a small projection at the end of each arm. They have conventional laurel leaves within a narrow raised edge, with an antique sword placed vertically, point uppermost, showing behind the central boss or medallion.

Above *Obverse Cross of Combatants Volunteers (FR.D016)* (Spink & Son Ltd)

The design of the reverse of the cross features plain arms, with narrow edges. The medallion has a circumscription, 'COMBATTANT VOLONTAIRE'. The centre of the medallion is adorned with a design of sun rays which are positioned above the dates 1939-1945.

The ribbon comprises a 38 mm red band, with 4 mm yellow side stripes inset by 1 mm, with a central green stripe which measures 8 mm.

FR.D017 Cross of Combatants Volunteers of the Resistance — 15 April 1954

This most attractive and unusual Cross was introduced on 15 April 1954 and comprises a straight-armed cross with a central boss or medallion. The tips of each arm have a small protrusion, while the arms have a raised edge which measures approximately 1 mm and runs round the arms of the cross and is carried on round the central boss. The fields of the arms of the cross are decorated with stylized laurel leaves, two sprays

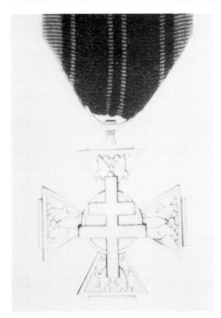

laurel berries and matching sized small triangles. The field of the medallion is plain and on to it is surmounted the Cross of Lorraine. The cross's arms are on the medallion and the upright arm that supports the crossbars is in the upper arm of the cross and the base is in the lower arm. The top of the cross has a small ball.

The reverse of the cross is plain except for the central boss or medallion which has the inscription, 'COMBATTANT VOLONTAIRE RESISTANCE', the first and second words being curved above and below the word 'RESISTANCE', which is positioned horizontally across the medallion.

The cross measures 36 mm across and is produced in gilded bronze. From the upper arm of the cross, on to the box protrusion, is placed an eyelet through which passes the ribbon ring, from which is a ribbon of black measuring 36 mm, with six red edge stripes measuring 5 mm and four green stripes, two in the centre spaced 2 mm apart and one on either side inset by 2 mm from the red edge. These measure 1.5 mm in width.

Above *Obverse Cross of Combatants Volunteers of the Resistance (FR.D017)* (Josef Charita)

on each arm, with three leaves in the bottom and four in the top spray. The other parts of the field not covered by the leaves are decorated with stylized

FR.D018 Medal of the French Resistance — 9 February 1943

General de Gaulle introduced this Medal on 9 February 1943 to reward the courage of members of the active Resistance. It comprises a round medal measuring 37 mm in diameter. The circumference has a raised edge approximately 2 mm in width; this edge rim is quite proud of the medal flan, leaving a recessed field. On to this field is surmounted a cross of Lorraine which is at the same level as the outer edge. The upright cuts this rim at the bottom and has a nick on either side to enhance its appearance

measures approximately 2 mm. On the field, on the left side of the cross beneath the lower arm, is the date in Roman numerals, XVIII.VI and on the other side, MCMXL, this date being that of the start of the German occupation of France.

The reverse has an inscription in large, sloping capitals, which is placed on a threefold scroll, the inscription being in Latin, 'PATRIA NON IMMEMOR', which translates to, 'The Fatherland is not Forgetful'. The medal is constructed in bronze that has been artificially patinated to a dark brown, nearly black, colour with the raised parts being polished to a bronze colour producing a contrast to the suspender, edge rim, cross and date.

Above *Obverse Medal of the French Resistance (FR.D018)* (Spink & Son Ltd)

The ribbon is black and measures 37 mm wide, with red edges measuring 4 mm and four 1 mm red stripes, two inset from the red edge by 2.5 mm and two central stripes 3 mm apart. For special cases, a rosette was authorized to be attached to the ribbon in November 1945.

while, at the top, it breaks the line of the edge and runs up above the medal by approximately 2 mm and on to its top is joined a trapezoid suspender. It has a flat configuration that matches the edge line and, once again,

FR.D019 Medal for Escaped Prisoners — 1926

This Medal was instituted in 1926 to reward prisoners who had escaped during the First World War and was made retroactive to encompass those prisoners who had escaped during the period of the Franco-Prussian War of 1870-1871. In the Second World War, however, it was not until 1944 that authorization for the bestowal of the medal was extended to encompass escapes during that conflict.

The Medal comprises a round medal with, as its obverse design, the head of a female looking to the right, the viewer's left. The portrait exhibits her neck and shoulders with a wreath placed around her head. The wreath is made up of an oak branch with its end tucked into a bun that she wears on the back of her head. This female head and torso was to represent emblematically the Republic of France. Her head and torso stand proud from

Above *Obverse The Médaille Militaire (FR.D009)* (Spink & Son Ltd)

Above right *Reverse Croix de Guerre (FR.D010) with plain central panel, made in London* (Josef Charita)

Right *Reverse Croix de Guerre (FR.D010). This Cross was cast in North Africa.*

Above left *Reverse Croix de Guerre 1939–1940 (FR.D011)*

Above *Reverse Croix de Guerre Overseas Theatre of Operations (FR.D013)* (Spink & Son Ltd)

Left *Reverse Cross of Combatants (FR.D014* (Josef Charita)

Above *Reverse Medal of the French Resistance (FR.D018)* (Spink & Son Ltd)

Above right *Reverse Medal for Escaped Prisoners (FR.D019)* (Spink & Son Ltd)

Right *Reverse Medal of Liberated France (FR.D020)*

Above left *Reverse Medal for those Deported or Interned for Political Reasons (FR.D022)*

Above *Obverse Free French Forces Medal (FR.D023)*

Left *Reverse Free French Forces Medal (FR.D023), manufacturer's variation* (Josef Charita)

the flat field of the medal on to which, in front, is the inscription 'REPUBLIQUE' and behind this 'FRANCAIS', the letters being raised from the field. The medal is constructed of bronze and the outline of the head and the legend are artificially patinated to give an outline or contrast to the motif and design.

The reverse again has a flat field on to which, round the edge, just inserted by approximately .5 mm, is a continuous wreath of oak leaves, comprising fourteen bunches in all, made up of three leaves to a bunch. These bunches are punctuated by two acorns. The central field has an inscription in capital letters positioned in three lines, one above the other, 'MEDAILLE, DES, EVADES'. This again is patinated to give a contrast to the design.

To the top of the medal is applied a ball suspender through which is placed the ribbon ring. The ribbon,

Above *Obverse Medal for Escaped Prisoners (FR.D019)* (Spink & Son Ltd)

in this case, comprises a 36 mm green band with a 7 mm wide central orange stripe, with a 2 mm wide orange side stripe inset by 2 mm.

FR.D020 Medal of Liberated France — 12 September 1947

This Medal was instituted on 12 September 1947 and comprises a round bronze medal that measures 35 mm in diameter. The obverse design has a flat field on to which is placed a map of France, upon which is placed the date 1944 in raised numerals. At the position on the map that represents the border between France and Spain and parallel to this in capital letters too small to be legible is found the designer's name.

Round the edge of the medal runs a large link chain that is broken by an eight-pointed star which has a central pellet and is in the relative position of Great Britain. From this emanate particles to emblematically represent a shellburst. There is a similar star at the bottom in the relative position of North Africa but, in this case, the star has seven points. Is this an allusion to the greater importance of General de Gaulle and the contribution of his forces to the liberation of France compared with that of General Giraud and the troops under his command stationed in North Africa?

The reverse design comprises a Phrygian Cap of Liberty surmounting a fasces. This has the initials 'R.F.' on either side and above and below 'LA FRANCE — À SES LIBÉRATEURS', in a curve.

There were a number of slight alterations to this Medal which was finally awarded to those persons, either French or Allied, who had not received the Legion of Honour (FR.D001-FR.D007), Medal of Gratitude (*), The Order of Liberation (FR.D008), Médaille Militaire (FR.D009) or Medal of the French Resistance (FR.D018), who had contributed a considerable effort towards the liberation of France. However, if the recipient had been awarded a medal such as one of the grades of the Legion of Honour or the Médaille Militaire for other military reasons apart from the liberation of France, it did not preclude those recipients from an award of this Medal. Thus by June 1955, 4,850 awards had been rendered to French nationals and 550 conferred upon foreigners.

Above *Obverse Medal of Liberated France (FR.D020)*

From the top of the medal is a round integral ball suspender, through which runs the ribbon ring. The design for the ribbon is taken from the Allied Victory Medal ribbon of 1914-1919. The design was reversed and consisted of a double rainbow merging.

FR.D021 Medal for those Deported or Interned for Acts of Resistance — 6 August 1948

This pentagonal Medal, constructed of bronze, was introduced on 6 August 1948 and comprises an obverse design that depicts flames at its centre, the field of the medal being flat. Superimposed on to the flames are crossed arms. The hand on the right arm is clenched while that on the left has its thumb and forefinger in the form of a 'V', emblematically to represent the victory of the Resistance fighters. Surmounting this is a chain, comprising fourteen links in all, that runs horizontally across the medal but stops at the edge of the flames, with half a broken link at each end.

The reverse design is made up of an inscription formed in six lines, 'REPUBLIQUE, FRANCAIS, MEDAILLE, DE LA DEPORTATION, ET DE L'INTERNEMENT, POUR FAITS DE RESISTANCE'. Beneath this is a Cross of Lorraine.

The medal measures 36 mm and has the point of the pentagon at the bottom, while the top has a box suspender for the ribbon. One of two Bars was applied to the ribbon, both comprising a design 44 mm long and 11 mm high, around which was a border approximately 2 mm in width with an inner recessed line. The field thus formed was further recessed and on to this, in large capital letters, was superimposed 'INTERNE' or 'DEPORTE'.

This medal was to reward those members of the Resistance who had been deported and subsequently imprisoned or sent to a concentration camp, or had been imprisoned or sent to a concentration camp in France itself. The period of incarceration that qualified the recipient was a minimum of three months, but this condition was waived if the recipient had escaped from the detention or had been executed while incarcerated.

The ribbon for the internees' medal comprises diagonal blue and white stripes which both measure 5 mm wide and run from top right to bottom left. The ribbon has a red edge stripe which measures 2 mm wide. That for the deported is made up of seven stripes measuring 5 mm wide, four blue and three white, with a red edge stripe 2 mm wide.

Below *Obverse Medal for those Deported or Interned for Acts of Resistance (FR.D021)* (Spink & Son Ltd)

FR.D022 Medal for those Deported or Interned for Political Reasons — 8 September 1948

This striking Medal was introduced on 8 September 1948 and comprised a round medal produced in bronze. The design of the obverse is very intricate and consists of a flat field on which, at the centre, is a small map of France. From the position on the map of the Brittany coast and Belgian border, emanate two shafts of light comprising four rays of variant widths. These stop short of the edge of the medal and, at this point, is found the inscription, 'REPUB-LIQUE FRANCAIS'. Beneath the words is a large chain link on its edge, that breaks the medal's rim and rises by 4 mm, on to which is positioned a trapezoid suspender. From the bottom of the link is joined a square link that encompasses the map of France and superimposes the rays. From the map then emanate four more shafts of light. Two run horizontally across the medal made up of five variable-width rays running downwards in a fan form which nearly touch the edge of the medal. Two pellets are then placed on the rim which separate the other two shafts from their predecessors on either side but, in this case, they are made up of four rays of similar appearance. Centrally, running from the bottom of the square chain, is a matching chain to that found in the upper section of the medal but, in this case, it only breaks the lower line of the medal by 2 mm. This is separated on either side by two

pellets from the shafts of light. These four lower shafts superimpose the square, central chain link.

The reverse design has a similar chain but, in this instance, it is broken on either side by the dates 1940-1945. It has an inscription round the edge, 'MEDAILLE DE LA DEPORTATION ET DE L'IN-TERNEMENT'.

Identical Bars to those worn on the ribbon of FR.D021 apply to this Medal, which was to recognize those French nationals who had been sub-jected to deportation or internment

Below *Obverse Medal for those Deported or Interned for Political Reasons (FR.D022)*

as political prisoners by the German occupational government or that of the Vichy government.

The ribbon for the internees' medal comprises diagonal blue and white stripes, both measuring 5 mm in width and running from top right to bottom left, bordered by a yellow edge stripe that measures 2 mm in width. That of the deported is made up of seven stripes, 5 mm wide, four blue and three white, bordered by yellow edge stripes that measure 2 mm in width.

FR.D023 Free French Forces Medal — 4 April 1946

This Medal was introduced on 4 April 1946 and takes the form of a Cross of Lorraine which is silver in colour. The cross has a recessed line that runs round the edge and is

Below *Obverse Free French Forces Medal (FR.D023), manufacturer's variation* (Josef Charita)

Below right *Reverse Free French Forces Medal (FR.D023)*

recessed by 1 mm. The field of the cross is flat and on to this, on the upper arm is, in capital letters, 'FRANCE', and on the lower arm, in similar capital letters, 'LIBRE'. These and the lines are patinated to give an antiqued appearance. The reverse is similar but with the dates '18 JUIN 1940-8 MAI 1945'.

From the top of the upper arm of the cross is a rectangular box from

which the ribbon is suspended. The medal was to reward those who had, before 1 August 1943, volunteered to serve in the Free French Forces or before 3 June 1943 had served in territories administered by the French National Committee.

The design of the ribbon com-prises a 38 mm royal blue band, with red diagonal stripes that measure 2 mm in width and are spaced 7 mm apart, running from top right to bottom left. When the ribbon was worn on the undress tunic, a minia-ture emblem of the cross was worn on it.

FR.D024 War Medal 1939-1945 — 21 May 1946

Introduced on 21 May 1946, this Medal comprises a pear-shaped hex-agon constructed of bronze. The obverse design has an outer edge rim approximately 2 mm thick running round the medal. The recessed field produced has a Cross of Lorraine. The top of the cross' upright super-imposes the edge line at the upper part of the medal, while the base joins the bottom edge line of the lower 'V' of the hexagon. Thus, the Cross of Lorraine gives the impression of tilt-ing forwards, while the tips of the upper arm of the cross partially rest on the edge line, and the lower ones touch. At this point the designer's name is found running from either side towards the centre in capital letters too small to be legible. The ends of the arms of the cross are bulbous and kidney-shaped. The base has a length of chain which forms a ground, on to which is placed a stylized Gallic cock which superim-poses the cross facing to the left, its head raised in a crowing position.

From the top of the medal is a stirrup suspender with a flat line measuring approximately 2 mm that complements the edge line. The design of the reverse comprises an inscription round the four upper sides of the medal, 'REPUBLIQUE

Below *Obverse War Medal 1939-1945 (FR.D024)*

FRANCAIS'. At the centre of the medal is a small laurel spray, beneath which is 'GUERRE, 1939, 1945', in three lines.

There were sixteen silver Bars issued to indicate the area of campaign or theatre of operation. Although two of these are not relevant to this work I have included them at the end of the listing for regularity. They all consist of a box 45 mm long and 10 mm high, with a raised convex edge line 2 mm wide. There is an inner line slightly recessed. The convexed edge is finely lined or grained. The field is recessed and on to this, in raised capitals, are the relevant inscriptions.

Bar

1 France
2 Norvège (Norway)
3 Afrique (Africa)
4 Italie (Italy)
5 Libération
6 Allemagne (Germany)
7 Grande Bretagne (Great Britain)
8 Atlantique (Atlantic)
9 Méditerranée (Mediterranean)
10 Mawcha
11 Mer du Nord (North Sea)
12 Défense Passive
13 Engagé Volontaire
14 Red enamelled five-pointed Star — War Wounds — Instituted 8 November 1952
15. (Extrême-Orient (Far East) 7.12.1941 — 15.8.1945)
16 (URSS (USSR) 28.11.1942 — 8.5.1945)

Period of qualification

1 — 3.9.1939 — 5.6.1940
2 — 12.4.1940 — 17.6.1940
3 — 25.6.1940 — 13.5.1943

Above *Reverse War Medal 1939-1945 (FR.D024)*

4 — 1.12.1943 — 25.7.1944
5 — 25.6.1940 — 8.5.1945
6 — 14.9.1944 — 8.5.1945
7 — 28.11.1942 — 8.5.1945
15 — 7.12.1941 — 15.8.1945
16 — 28.11.1942 — 8.5.1945

The medal was to commemorate the service the recipient had rendered during the 1939-1945 war and was awarded to French personnel who had been in an official French unit or that of an Allied army, navy or air force unit. In certain cases it was possible for a civilian to become eligible for the award, such as fishermen who had become engaged in the war effort.

Notes: The Italie Bar was for operations in Italy and Elba but was withdrawn with the introduction of the Italian Campaign 1943-1944 Medal (FR.D025) described below from 1

April 1953. The Grande Bretagne Bar was for involvement from Great Britain in aerial operations that had taken place between the qualifying dates. The Atlantique and Méditerranée Bars were to reward maritime operations in the requisite vicinities represented by the individual bar.

The design of the ribbon comprises a 38 mm light blue band with edge bands of 4 mm green, with 1 mm red edges, while down the centre of the band were placed a series of 4 mm high red 'V's.

FR.D025 Italian Campaign 1943-1944 Medal — 1 April 1953

This Medal was instituted rather belatedly on 1 April 1953 and is a silver medal constructed in bronze which measures 36 mm in diameter. The obverse design comprises a wreath of laurel leaves, two side by side, which measure 4 mm in width. The wreath is broken by a ribbon cross at 12, 3, 6 and 9 o'clock. The quadrants thus formed each have four pairs of laurel leaves, with a laurel berry at the base and apex of each, giving five berries in each quadrant. Within the wreath is a central boss or medallion which has a circumscription that starts and ends with a five-pointed star, 'CORPS EXPEDITIONNAIRE FRANCAIS D'ITALIE'. Between the stars are the dates 1943-1944. The central field has sun rays emanating from a horizon that runs horizontally inset from the beginning and ending of the inscription. On to this, surmounting the sun rays, is a right-facing, strutting Gallic cock in the action of crowing.

The reverse design has a similar laurel wreath border, with a circumscription, 'REPUBLIQUE FRANCAIS', and a five-pointed star below

Below   *Obverse   Italian   Campaign 1943–1944 Medal (FR.D025)*

which contains, at its centre, 'CEF' formed in a monogram.

This Medal was to reward members of the French Expeditionary Corps who, between 1 December 1943 and 25 July 1944, had served in Italy or the Isle of Elba. With the introduction of this medal, the Bar of FR.D024 was discontinued and withdrawn.

The ribbon comprised a 39 mm wide band, made up of thirteen equal stripes of red and white, seven in the former colour and six in the latter.

French Air Force Wings

FR.A001 French Air Force Pilots' Badge — 10 September 1916

The badge was instituted on 10 September 1916 and consists of a circular oak leaf wreath with a ribbon bow at its base. Surmounting its apex is a five-pointed star with the single point uppermost. The arms of the star each have a raised central spine that culminate together at a single point midway of the body of the star. Across the badge is a pair of wings that curve inwards and form a 'V' at the centre. The upper part of the 'V' is raised and below this is the illusion of downy feathers that are situated on either side as the first line of fletching. Two rows of pin feathers in a fan formation, butting together with an inverted 'V' of feathers, run beneath. The middle row of feathers, or the first line below the downy layer, consist of ten pin feathers on the right and nine on the left. The lower row has eleven and ten feathers respectively. From the top of this lower line of pin feathers are seven gently upward-sweeping horizontal lines of fletching on the right, and eight on the left.

The badge can be encountered manufactured in one of three methods, either as a one-, two- or three-piece construction. The wreath can be a separate entity, the wings can be applied separately as can the star, or the star and wreath can be struck as one integral piece, on to which the wings are separately applied. The one-piece construction entails the whole badge being produced in one integral die strike.

The wings and star are gilt and the wreath is silver. The reverse has two eyelets through which is placed a retaining pin. A number is also found which may have the prefix 'G.B.', indicating a newly-qualified free French pilot trained in Great Britain. An 'A' prefix to represent Africa is also found for, after the fall of France in 1940, the French pilot schools were relocated in Morocco and continued to issue flying badges.

It is worn on the right breast, just above the tunic pocket. A point of

Below *French Air Force Pilots' Badge (FR.A001)*

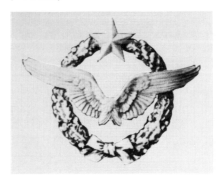

interest is that this badge has perceivably the longest history of continuous award and use with no design change of any pilots' badge, and is still employed by the French Air Force today.

FR.A002 French Air Force Student Pilots' Badge — 1924-1948

This badge was introduced in 1916 but the French Air Force redesignated its flying badges in 1924. To keep in step with established works of reference I have tabulated the badges in a like manner. This badge comprises a wreath identical in format to that of the Pilots' Badge (FR.A001) but, in this case, the star has been removed from the apex of the wreath and incorporated into the wing design. This is a half wing with the five-pointed star positioned at the wing's root. The overall colour of the badge is silver. It is of two-piece construction and measures 43 mm wingtip to wreath and 36 mm vertically. The reverse is plain with similar eyelets for attachment to the tunic and reference number. It is

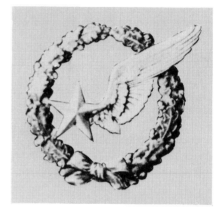

Above *French Air Force Student Pilots' Badge (FR.A002)*

worn on the right breast, just above the tunic pocket.

FR.A003 French Air Force Observers' Badge — 1924

This badge was also introduced in 1916 and redesignated in 1924. It takes the form of the preceding badge (FR.A002) but, in this case, the star and wing are of gilt and the wreath is silver. The badge is of identical two-piece construction and size, with similar eyelets and an issue number on the reverse. It is worn on the right breast, just above the tunic pocket.

FR.A004 French Air Force Airship Pilots' Badge — 1924

This badge is identical to FR.A001 except for the fact that the star is replaced by a steering wheel that has four spokes. It is produced in a three-part construction and measures 55 mm wingtip to wingtip and 42 mm from the base of the bow to the top of the steering wheel. The steering wheel is to represent airship or balloon personnel. The colour of the wheel and the wings is gilt while the wreath is silver.

The reverse has eyelets for attachment as previously described but, in this case, the badges are usually unnumbered and devoid of manufacturers' marks. The badge is worn on the right breast, just above the tunic

Above *French Air Force Airship Pilots' Badge (FR.A004)*

pocket, as with the other flying awards.

FR.A005 French Air Force Airship Student Pilots' Badge — 1924

This badge is identical to FR.A002 with the exception that the star has been replaced by the steering wheel. The colours are also identical in that the steering wheel, wing and wreath are all silver. The badge is of a two-

piece construction and measures 43 mm wingtip to wreath and 36 mm vertically. The reverse is plain with similar eyelets for attachment to the tunic, it being worn on the right breast, just above the tunic pocket.

FR.A006 French Air Force Airship Mechanics' or Observers' Badge — 1924

This badge is identical to FR.A003, with the exception that the star has

been replaced by the steering wheel. The colours are also identical, in that

the steering wheel and wing are gilt and the wreath is silver. The badge is of a two-piece construction and measures 43 mm wingtip to wreath and 36 mm vertically. The reverse is plain with similar eyelets for attachment to the tunic, and the reference number. It is worn on the right breast, just above the tunic pocket.

Left *French Air Force Airship Mechanics' or Observers' Badge (FR.A006)*

FR.A007 French Air Force Aircrew Badge — 1924

This badge was first introduced in 1916 but redesignated in 1924 and was to recognize bombardiers, machine-gunners, mechanics and photographers who were employed in either aircraft or airships. The badge is circular and reminiscent of a bicycle tyre with no treads. On to this is placed a two-bladed propeller with a single wing attached, at its root, to the boss. The badge was produced in a two-part construction, measures 38 mm horizontally and 50 mm vertically and is of an overall silver colour. The reverse is plain with the similar eyelets for attachment to the tunic, and the award number. It is worn on the right breast, just above the tunic pocket.

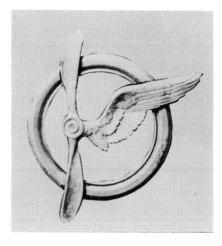

Above *French Air Force Aircrew Badge (FR.A007)*

French Naval Flying Badges

FR.N001 French Naval Seaplane Pilots' Badge — 18 April 1917

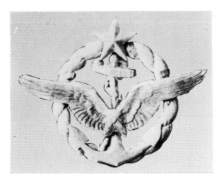

Above *French Naval Seaplane Pilots' Badge* *(FR.N001)*

The design of this badge comprises a wreath formed of twisted rope. On to this is a large anchor that surmounts the rope wreath at the bottom, its top joining the wreath at its apex. Placed across the badge is a pair of wings identical to those found in FR.A001 and a five-pointed star at the wreath's apex. The badge is produced in three parts, wreath and anchor, wings and the star. The colour of the last two parts is gilt while the main body of the badge, which comprises the wreath and anchor, is silver. It is worn on the tunic in the same manner as the former Air Force badges.

FR.N002 French Naval Aircrew Badge — 1940

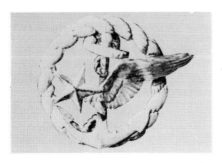

Above *French Naval Aircrew Badge* *(FR.N002)*

This badge comprises a similar rope wreath and anchor but has a five-pointed star attached at the root of a single wing. This badge is of a two-part construction consisting of a gilt star and wing and silver wreath and anchor. The badge was secured to the tunic by the two eyelets and was worn on the tunic in the same place as the former Air Force badges.

FR.N003 French Naval Airship Pilots' Badge for Officers with Licence — 18 April 1917

This badge is identical to FR.N001 but has the star removed and replaced by the steering wheel, as is the case in FR.A004. The colours are also the same. This badge was to reward officers with a captain's licence. The badge is of a three-part construction and secured to the tunic by the two eyelets and was worn in the same place as the former Air Force badges.

Right *French Naval Airship Pilots' Badge for Officers with Licence (FR.N003)*

FR.N004 French Naval Airship Steering Pilots' Badge

This badge is identical to the French Naval Air Crew Badge (FR.N002) but with the replacement of the star by the steering wheel. It was to recognize the personnel who were also employed as airship mechanics, airship radio telegraphists, airship machine-gunners and balloon observers but, in this case, the badge was also awarded to the observers of static balloons. It is of two-part construction and secured to the tunic by the two eyelets, and was worn in the same place as the former Air Force badges.

Above *French Naval Airship Steering Pilots' Badge (FR.N004)*

FR.N005 Free French Naval Pilots' Badge — 1942

This badge was produced in Great Britain by the Gaunt firm and is identical in every respect to FR.N003 but with the addition of a small gold Cross of Lorraine placed on the anchor's stock.

Right *Free French Naval Pilots' Badge (FR.N005)*

FR.N006 Free French Naval Aircrew Badge — 1942

This badge was produced, like the previous one, by the Gaunt firm and is identical to FR.N002 but with the addition of a small gold Cross of Lorraine on the anchor's stock.

Left *Free French Naval Aircrew Badge (FR.N006)*

Awards of the Netherlands armed forces

Holland was invaded on 10 May 1940 without any formal declaration of war, but the attack was not altogether unexpected. The Dutch capitulated on 14 May. A number of exiles moved to Britain, including Queen Wilhelmina and the entire Dutch government and a considerable number of Dutch soldiers. These soldiers were formed into the Royal Dutch Brigade, which later became the Princess Irene Brigade.

About 250 men, including eight instructors and eighty trainees from the training school of Flushing and Haamsted, arrived in Britain at the end of May 1940, via France. At approximately the same time the crews of eight aeroplanes of the Naval Air Service crossed the Channel to Britain. From these small beginnings the Netherlands Armed Forces were slowly rebuilt in Britain and during the course of the war, a new Dutch Air Force was reorganized. Some ships of the Dutch Navy also made it to British ports. These were strengthened by ships from Great Britain and later vessels obtained from the United States. The number of personnel in this marine corps reached 6,500 officers and men, who served both in the Dutch Navy and the Dutch Reserve. The Dutch merchant marine was of considerable size and the bulk of this force was able to evade internment by the Germans and side with the Allies. The Dutch Resistance also played a valuable part in the war effort, particularly in the repatriation of British aircrew.

Index to Dutch Awards

Dutch Army Air Service Wings

Dutch Naval Air Service Wings

British awards to Dutch nationals

	Medal	1st Bar
GB.D006 The Distinguished Service Cross	41	2
GB.D007 The Distinguished Service Medal	44	
GB.D009 Military Cross	8	
GB.D010 Military Medal	9	
GB.D011 The Distinguished Conduct Medal	1	
GB.D012 The Distinguished Flying Cross	43	1
GB.D013 The Air Force Cross	2	
GB.D014 The Conspicuous Gallantry Medal (Flying)	1	
GB.D015 The Distinguished Flying Medal	7	

Military Order of William

This Order is the highest and only award for the kingdom of Holland and is therefore tied tightly to the crown. The monarch is the head of the Order, which is awarded in four grades. The background and history is not relevant to this work so suffice it to say that it was originally introduced by King William I on 30 April 1815.

It was inaugurated to reward military personnel who had rendered to the monarch, and thus the state, deeds of outstanding courage, leadership or loyalty, or a combination of all three. It is possible to award the order to civilians and foreign nationals under the same conditions, but it is very rarely conferred at all, and thus is highly coveted. When recipients wear the Order they are saluted by those who have not been awarded it or by the recipients of the lower grades of the order. It also has another unusual feature from the British standpoint, in the fact that an individual who feels that he or she is worthy of bestowal of the Order, may apply for its award. The Order also carries with it the provision for a pension. In 1940 a rosette was authorized to be added to the Knights Third Class ribbon.

The status of the Order was reviewed and restructured on 30 June 1941 and these are the relevant decrees that cover the Second World War. During its period of manufacture there have been design changes which are mainly attributable to variations in craftsmanship. The descriptions of the medals that follow are relevant to the Orders found during the period of the Second World War and the descriptions should be seen in that context.

NE.D001 Military Order of William — Grand Cross — Star — 30 June 1941

This grade is also referred to as Knights First Class and comprises a badge of the Order which is worn on a sash, which itself has a sash badge (see below) suspended from a bow which is formed at the joining of the two ends of the band.

The Star is eight-pointed, and on it is mounted the badge of the Order. The star is convex and produced in silver. Four arms are at the relative positions of 1, 3, 6 and 9 o'clock and are produced of seven pencil rays, while those between are of five, but their tips form a symmetrical configuration around the outside. The central ray of each arm has a pelleted outline and a raised inner spine which is smooth.

Adjacent to this, both rays have a similar border but the inner pencil is flat with engraved overlapping sequins as its design. The rays next to these repeat the design of the central pencil ray. Each ray is terminated with a round ball finial. The central design comprises a Maltese cross with a chamfered edge and, at each tip, a ball finial. The inner field is of white opaque enamel, with the inscription in capital letters, 'VOOR MOED BELEID TROUW', one word on each arm of the cross. This translates as 'For courage, leadership, loyalty'.

Between the arms of the cross are crossed Burgundian branches or ragged staffs. These comprise four triangles in each quadrant. They are set into one another and give the impression of a stylized Christmas tree. The outer one has a base with five protrusions. Each of these has small lines in the field which number four or five. The whole of the field is filled with green transparent enamel. The whole of the design of the cross has a thin outline. On the centre surmounting the whole cross is a tinder box, which also has a raised edge and the field in the centre has horizontal lines.

All the metal parts exposed on the central cross are gilded and polished. The reverse has a large pin for securing the insignia to the sash or tunic.

NE.D002 Military Order of William — Grand Cross — Sash Badge — 30 June 1941

This insignia is identical in construction to the central badge of the Star, save that the upper arm of the cross has an inverted plain 'V' with a hinged crown attached. The construction of the crown comprises five arches which have a number of pearls or pellets attached. The arches are segmented and from the apex of these is positioned an orb with a cross. Through the orb is placed a large ring which enables the badge to be hooked on to the sash by means of a hook which has a hinged side. The reverse of the cross has a crowned 'W'

for its founder William which is on a blue enamelled boss or medallion, surrounded by a laurel wreath.

The sash is a band 101 mm wide of a watered orange-yellow overall colour with, inset by 10 mm, a blue stripe 15 mm wide.

NE.D003 Military Order of William — Commander — 30 June 1941

This is also referred to as the Knights Second Class and comprises a breast star which is worn on the left breast and a cross which is worn suspended from a ribbon around the neck.

The star is identical to that described in NE.D001, while the neck badge is the same as the Grand Cross Sash Badge (NE.D002) and the

Knights Third Class (NE.D004) since the same insignia is used in the varying grades in combination with the star. It has a ribbon of the same colours and proportions as those of the Grand Cross Sash but, in this case, the ribbon measures 55 mm wide.

NE.D004 Military Order of William — Knights Third Class — 30 June 1941

This is identical in design to the Grand Cross Sash Badge (NE.D002). It is worn with a ribbon of the same design as the previous neck ribbon but, in this case, a rosette is added to the ribbon which measures 37 mm of orange yellow with 5 mm Nasau blue side stripes inset by 5 mm. The insignia is worn on the left breast.

Obverse Military Order of William - Knights Third Class (NE.D004) (Spink & Son Ltd)

NE.D005 Military Order of William — Knights Fourth Class — 30 June 1941

This is again identical in design to the Grand Cross Sash Badge (NE.D002) but, in this case, the whole body of the insignia is silver save for the legend, 'VOOR MOED BELEID TROUW' and the tinderbox which are gilded as is the 'W' on the reverse.

The ribbon is of the same size and design as the aforementioned one but no rosette is applied in this instance. The cross is worn on the left breast.

NE.D006 Resistance Cross — 3 May 1946

This Cross was instituted on 3 May 1946 and consists of a Latin cross with straight, slightly widening, arms, measuring 60 mm by 36 mm, the lower arm being longer than the others. Between the angles of the

Obverse Resistance Cross (NE.D006)

Reverse Resistance Cross (NE.D006)

arms are rays. St George spearing the dragon comprises the design at the centre, while the arms of the cross have an inscription 'TROUW TOT IN DEN DOOD', which translates as 'Faithful unto Death'. This inscription is read from the top, then left to right and finishes at the bottom. The reverse design comprises a flaming sword and two broken handcuffs. From the upper arm of the cross is a stylized crown with an orb at the top through which passes the ribbon suspension ring. The overall construction of the medal is of bronze.

This medal was given in recognition to those members of the Resistance who performed feats of outstanding courage and leadership during the German occupation which ran from 10 May 1940 to 7 May 1945.

The ribbon is crimson, 37 mm wide, with side stripes of yellow which measure 4 mm wide and are inset by 4 mm.

NE.D007 Resistance Cross Posthumous — 3 May 1946

This Cross was instituted like the previous award on 3 May 1946 and takes exactly the same design, except that the cross is larger, measuring 80 mm by 48 mm. It was awarded under the same conditions but to reward those members of the Resistance who had perished by one means or another during the occupation. It was presented to the next of kin in direct line of descent.

NE.D008 The Honourable Mention — 8 September 1877

The history of this emblem will not be discussed at this point. It was discontinued and replaced by the introduction on 30 March 1944 of the Bronze Lion (NE.D009).

During the Second World War the emblem was worn on either the ribbon of either the Flying Cross (NE.D010), or the ribbon of the Bronze Cross (NE.D011). Prior to their institution it had been worn on the ribbon of the Expedition Cross, which is not covered in this work. It was to reward a near miss of the Military Order of William, when the recipient had been cited in an Order of the Day for an act of bravery. Thus this emblem, which comprises a small silver gilt crown, ranked second only to that of the Military Order of William.

NE.D009 The Bronze Lion — 30 March 1944

This Cross was instituted on 30 March 1944 by Queen Wilhelmina and comprises a cross patté in bronze. The arms of the cross have a raised outer edge and there is a large central boss or medallion. This circle has a matching outer line, the field produced between these lines (that is to say, those of the arms of the cross and those of the central boss) being finely pebbled. On the central field is superimposed the rampant lion of the Netherlands, crowned and holding a sword in its right paw and a bundle of arrows in its left. The reverse is plain. From the upper arm of the cross is an unusual suspender, that protrudes into the field of the upper arm, then runs upwards and has a stirrup ribbon eyelet, through which passes the ribbon. The whole of the cross, including the suspender, is patinated with the flat or smooth surfaces of the cross polished, which gives a striking contrast to the matt areas which comprise the fields of the cross.

This Cross was to reward officers and NCOs of the armed forces of the Netherlands, civilian members of her Merchant Marine, as well as foreign personnel who had distinguished themselves during the war by occasioning acts of heroism or leadership

Obverse Bronze Lion (NE.D009)

in the face of the enemy, and was to replace the Honourable Mention (NE.D008). It thus became the highest gallantry award of the Netherlands. For subsequent awards, Arabic numbers relevant to the award were applied to the ribbon. These numerals measure approximately 12 mm high and are produced in bronze.

The ribbon consists of nine equal-size stripes, five of Nassau blue and four of orange.

NE.D010 Flying Cross — 28 August 1941

This Cross is also referred to as the Airman's Cross and was instituted on

28 August 1941. It is of a design that is referred to as a Teutonic or Victo-

Obverse Dutch Flying Cross (NE.D010)

ria Cross, that is to say that the arms of the cross radiate out in a straight line to a large, flat top. The centre has a large central boss or medallion. The edges of the cross are outlined with a polished, raised line. The boss is likewise outlined and has a similar inner line. The field of the arms of the cross are pebbled, while the field of the boss is plain. The upper arm has a five-arched crown surmounting it and resting directly on to the edge of the boss. A flying eagle reminiscent of that used by the RAF is placed across the horizontal arms of the cross, with its wingtips just breaking

the edge line of each side. In the 'tramlines' above the body of the eagle is the word 'INITIA-TIEFMOED', and on the central field below it the date, 1941. Beneath the body of the eagle in the 'tramline' is the word 'VOLHARDING'. The inscription translates as 'Initiative, Courage, Perseverance'.

The reverse is plain except, in some cases, for the sterling silver mark as the Cross was produced in silver in Great Britain.

The Cross was intended to reward those members of the Netherlands flying forces as well as her allies who had, during combat as well as in general air duties against the enemy, performed acts of initiative, courage or perseverance. It could also be awarded to civilians and conferred posthumously upon a deserving recipient.

The upper arm has an integral ball suspender through which runs a ribbon ring. Through this is placed the 30 mm wide white ribbon, on to which are set 3.5 mm wide stripes of orange which run diagonally downwards from left to right. Any subsequent bestowal of the award is represented by the addition to the ribbon of the appropriate Roman numeral, executed in gold.

NE.D011 Bronze Cross — 11 June 1940

This Cross was introduced by Queen Wilhelmina on 11 June 1940 and again comprised a Teutonic or Victoria Cross design executed in bronze.

The central boss forms the dominant part of the design and the arms of the cross are enveloped into it by the use of a raised outer edge that, in this

Obverse Bronze Cross (NE.D011) (Spink & Son Ltd)

Reverse Bronze Cross (NE.D011) (Spink & Son Ltd)

case, runs continuously round the arms and the boss. The boss, or medallion, has a wreath of laurel leaves and oak leaves, the former on the left and the latter on the right. This is tied at the base with a ribbon tie, while the apex is open. Into this gap is placed a five-arched crown, while the centre is adorned by a capital 'W'.

The reverse bears the date 1940 in a laurel and oak leaf wreath, while on the arms of the cross is the inscription, 'TROUW AAN KONINGIN EN VADERLAND', which translates as 'True to Queen and Country'. This award originally ranked below the Honourable Mention (NE.D008) but, after the introduc-

tion of the Bronze Lion (NE.D009) which superseded it, beneath that, and was intended to reward members of the Army and Navy, as well as civilians and members of the Allied forces who had not warranted the award of the equivalent higher decoration, in either of its forms, for acts of courage or by leadership in the face of the enemy.

From the upper arm, to which an integral ball is fitted, runs a ribbon ring. This has an orange-yellow ribbon with a narrow central blue stripe. For subsequent awards Arabic numerals which relate to the number of times the award has been bestowed are fixed on to the ribbon.

NE.D012 Cross of Merit — 20 February 1941

Queen Wilhelmina introduced on 20 February 1941 a bronze cross with straight arms (ie, the angle of the arms are at 90 degrees to one another). Inset 1 mm on to each of the arms is a raised edge of approximately 1 mm which runs round the whole of the cross. A laurel wreath is superimposed on the cross running from the lower arm, where the twigs cross one into each corner of the inner line. The wreath then breaks the arms of the cross and runs upwards through the horizontal arm on either side, passing through the upper arm, just breaking the inner line on either side. The wreath is constructed of leaves, three together, separated from the next bunch by two

Reverse Cross of Merit (NE.D012) (Spink & Son Ltd)

Obverse Cross of Merit (NE.D012) (Spink & Son Ltd)

laurel berries, there being seven bunches in all. To the centre of the cross is a capital 'W', which has a flat line at the top of each leg. One of each is placed just inside the horizontal arm, while the upturned 'V' is positioned in the lower arm and situated just above this is a five-arched crown.

The reverse design is plain and depicts a small rampant Dutch lion at its centre, with a curved inscription, 'VOOR VERDIENSTE', above and below it, which translates as 'For Merit'.

The upper arm has a flat box suspender, through which runs the ribbon. The area between the angle of the arms of the cross and the inner edge of the wreath is segmented.

This award was intended for those Dutchmen as well as foreign subjects, both military and civilian, who had acted in the interests of the Netherlands by distinguishing themselves by courageous and resolute behaviour during enemy action.

The ribbon comprises a 25 mm wide Nassau blue band with a 5 mm central orange yellow stripe.

NE.D013 Medal of Gratitude — Silver Class — February 1946
NE.D014 Medal of Gratitude — Bronze Class — February 1946

Both Medals are of identical design and represent different degrees of indebtedness of the Dutch people. The medals were instituted in February 1946 and comprise a round medal, measuring 29 mm in diameter, round the edge of which is an inscription in Latin, 'SIBI BENEFACIT QUI BENEFACIT AMICO', which translates as 'He helps himself, who helps a friend'. The central design is of Androcles and the Lion, an allusion to the lion of Holland, and depicts Androcles extracting the thorn from the lion's foot.

The medal has, at its top, a stylized crown with an orb surmounting it, through which is placed the ribbon suspension ring. The reverse design also has an inscription, again in Latin, which reads 'POPULUS BATAVUS GRATO ANIMO', which translates as 'The Dutch People in Gratitude'. The central design is a rampant lion holding a bundle of arrows in one paw and a sword in the other, the emblem of Holland.

These medals were to reward individuals, particularly those who had not been recognized by the award of

Obverse Medal of Gratitude - Silver Class (NE.D013)

an order of knighthood, who had occasioned acts or meritorious service to the Dutch ideals or affairs, during the period of the occupation 1940-1945. It was also bestowed for acts of outstanding assistance to Dutch personnel during the time of conflict of the Second World War.

The ribbon comprises an orange-yellow band with a narrow white central stripe.

Reverse Medal of Gratitude - Bronze Class (NE.D014)

NE.D015 War Commemorative Cross 1940-1945 — 16 March 1944

This Cross was instituted by Queen Wilhelmina on 16 March 1944 and has an oval boss as its central design. This has, as its outline, a belt or garter with a buckle at the relative position of 7 o'clock, on to which is the inscription 'VOOR KRIJGSVER-RICHTINGEN', which translates as 'For War Operations'. The central field is plain with a bust of Queen Wilhelmina facing right, left to the viewer. From the belt or garter radiate four arms of a cross at the relative positions of 12, 6, 3 and 9 o'clock which widen to just over twice the width at their ends. These

ends are cut across and the tops are slightly concave. The edge is raised and the field is flat and on to this is applied a 'W' made up of two overlapping 'V's, one on each arm. Between the angles of the cross is an oak leaf wreath, made up of two lines of leaves, the outer row having acorns interspersed between them. This wreath is in lower relief than the central oval boss and the arms of the cross. Thus, they give the impression that they are superimposed upon it. From the upper arm is a semi-circular loop. The raised parts of the cross are polished bronze while the lower relief portions are of patinated bronze. The reverse is plain and dark bronze in colour.

There are a number of Bars authorized for individual actions or campaigns. The basic Bar for each has an identical design comprising a bar, with rounded ends and raised edges with scrolled ends. The rounded ends have eight small rays emanating from the scrolls. Two small panels are placed on to the bar, with 'V'-shaped ends, and it is on to these panels that was placed, in small capital letters, the relevant information relating to the action or campaign that the Bar commemorated. The field on the bar was very lightly pebbled.

Twelve of these Bars were authorized and those relevant to this theatre are as follows:

(a) KRIJGTER ZEE 1940-1945 (War at Sea); (b) OORLOGS-VLUCHTEN 1940-1945 (War Flights); (c) OORLOGSDIENST KOOPVAARDIJ 1940-1945 (War Service Merchant Navy); (d) OOR-LOGSDIENSTVISSERIJ 1940-1945 (War Service Fishery); (e) KRIJGTE LAND 1940-1945 (War on Land); (f) NEDERLAND MEI 1940 (Holland May 1940); (g) NOORD AFRIKA-ITALIE 1941-1942; (h) MIDDELLANDSE ZEE 1940-1945 (Mediterranean Sea); (i) A R N H E M - N I J M E G E N - WALCHEREN 1944; and (j) NOR-MANDIE 1944. Three more bars were authorized but these were for the Japanese campaign: (k) NEDERLANDSCH-INDIE 1941-1942 (Dutch East Indies); (l) JAVA-ZEE 1941-1942 (Java Sea); and (m) O O S T - A Z I E - Z U I D - P A C I F I C 1942-1945 (East Asia South Pacific).

I have listed thirteen Bars, while only initially stating that there were twelve. This apparent mistake is accounted for by the fact that on 6 January 1948 (g) was replaced by (h) but it is possible to encounter (g) although it is not, from that date, a recognized award. It is also possible to find (k) in a different spelling.

This Cross was to reward war service in its broadest connotations and was most successful in this operation with the use of the various Bars. Service with the Allies in ships that were registered to Holland or the Dutch Indies military or civilian air force, rendered the personnel eligible for the award and bestowal of a relevant Bar or Bars. The ground crews of the Dutch air arms were also eligible, under the same conditions. However, only one Bar for general operations, a, b, c, d or e, could be worn with the Cross.

The ribbon is 27 mm wide,

Obverse War Commemorative Cross 1940–1945 (NE.D015) (Spink & Son Ltd)

watered orange yellow, with side
stripes of green 5 mm wide. It is
curved round with the cross couched

in the centre. The double furled ribbon thus measures approximately 40
mm.

NE.D016 Mobilization Cross 1939-1945 — 11 August 1948

This Cross was instituted on 11
August 1948 and takes the form of a
cross with arms that widen from the
centre. The ends of the arms are cut in
gentle ellipses, which form a pointed
end to the cross. From the point to
the centre of the cross on each arm is
a raised ridge. At the cross' centre is a
Dutch steel helmet, around which
runs a palm wreath, diagonally from
left to right. The helmet also has three
pellets upon it. Through the angles of
the arms of the cross are placed
crossed double-edged swords. The
swords have plain hilts with six rings
on the handle and a knob pommel
with a pellet. Beneath the swords are
a number of rays which come out and
form a semi-circle. The upper arm of
the cross has a ball finial for the
ribbon suspender.

The reverse has a recessed central
circle containing the legend, 'DEN
VADERLANT   GHETROUWE',
which translates as 'Loyal to the
Fatherland'. The overall colour of the
cross is of patinated bronze.

This Cross was to reward those
personnel who did not qualify for the
War   Commemorative   Cross
(NE.D015) but had been members
of the Dutch forces who had served

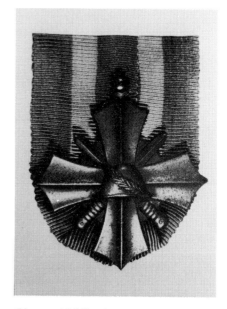

*Obverse Mobilization Cross 1939–1945
(NE.D016)* (Spink & Son Ltd)

during the mobilization from 6 April
1939, in fact before the actual start of
hostilities, and had subsequently
served during the ensuing war.

The ribbon design consisted of a
36 mm wide violet band, with a
central 6 mm orange stripe.

Dutch Army Air Service Wings
NE.A001 Army Air Service Pilots' Wings
(Cloth) — 14 October 1919

This badge was introduced on 14 October 1919 and comprises an eagle in flight superimposing an orange circle. The eagle is flying to the right (the viewer's left) and the design is executed in gold bullion with an orange base, all worked on to a blue backing. The orange circle has threads emanating from its centre to represent the sun's rays and is outlined with twisted gold wire. The eagle's wings have pointed tips broken by three lines of fletching, which gently curve round and join the other side. The right wing has seven lines of fletching and the left, nine. Thus the overall dimensions of the left wing are larger than that of the right. The eagle's body is streamlined into the wing configuration and the head is superimposed on to the right wing, with only the tip of

Army Air Service Pilots' Wings (NE.A001) (A. Forman)

the beak breaking the wing line.

This badge was used up until 1940 but probably was in service for longer than the allotted time. It measures 91 mm including the backing, wingtip to wingtip, and 32 mm high. Without the backing, wingtip to wingtip, the measurements are 80 mm and the circle measures 24 mm across. This was worn on the left breast, above the tunic pocket and any service ribbons.

NE.A002 Army Air Service Pilots' Wings
(Metal) — 1940

This badge was introduced in 1940. Some references state that the metal badge is the type produced in England. However, examples were made in Holland which bear the legend in two lines, 'KON BEARER, VOOR SCHOLEN'. Examples were produced in Britain by the firm of

Toye. These were produced in silver and bear the silver mark.

The general design is similar to that of the cloth version but is extremely well executed in either silver or gilded metal. It comprises an eagle in flight flying to the right (the viewer's left). The measurements are

86 mm wingtip to wingtip. This is superimposed over a circle that measures 23 mm and is surrounded by seventeen pellets on an edge border above the eagle and eighteen beneath. The field produced has raised rays, ten touching the border, five stopping 2 mm from the border and five stopping 3 mm from it in the area above the eagle, and similar numbers in the area beneath. The whole of the circle is enamelled in transparent orange. The upper edge of the wing is straight and dips, forming a 'V' at the truncation of the circle, and flows to the eagle's body, which is incorporated into the other wing. This upper edge is raised and has a line of 35 feathers, which stop at the upper line of the eagle's body. A similar line of feathers is found on the left-hand wing, which once again comprise 35 in number. Beneath this line, on the left-hand wing, are eight rows of straight fletching, which join three rows of downward-pointing

Army Air Service Pilots' Wings (NE.A002) (A. Forman)

feathers, twelve in the top row, sixteen in the middle row and seventeen in the lower row that produces the bottom line.

The eagle's head lays on this line, with its eye in the same relative position as the pellets that form the border. Its beak protrudes beneath the wing and breaks the pelleted circle. The opposite wing comprises seven straight lines of fletching, which join three rows of downward-pointing feathers that complement the opposite feathers but, in this case, all three rows have twelve.

The reverse is plain with only the logo, in two lines, or it can be found plain with a pin which is like half of a large safety pin. The gilt is matt on both the reverse and obverse of the badge. It was worn on the left breast above the tunic pocket and any service ribbons.

NE.A003 Army Air Service Pilot Observers' Wings (Cloth) — 30 December 1930

This badge was instituted on 30 December 1930 and takes exactly the

same design as the Pilots' Badge (NE.A001) but with the addition of a

Above *Obverse War Medal 1939–1945 (FR.D024), manufacturer's variation* (Josef Charita)

Above right *Reverse Italian Campaign 1943–1944 Medal (FR.D025)*

Right *Reverse Military Order of William – Knights Third Class (NE.D004)* (Spink & Son Ltd)

Above left *Obverse The Order of St Olaf –
Grand Cross Sash Badge on Sash
(NW.D001)* (Spink & Son Ltd)

Above *Obverse War Cross (NW.D006)*
(Spink & Son Ltd)

Left *Obverse The Order of Leopold – Grand
Officer – Breast Star with Swords
(BE.D011)* (Josef Charita)

Above *Reverse The Order of Leopold –
Commander – with Swords (BE.D014)*
(Josef Charita)

Above right *Obverse The Order of Leopold –
Officers (BE.D016)* (Josef Charita)

Right *Reverse The Order of Leopold –
Officers – with Swords (BE.D017)* (Josef
Charita)

Above left *Obverse The Order of Leopold -
Knights - with Swords (BE.D020)* (Josef
Charita)

Above *Reverse Military Cross First Class
(BE.D022)* (Josef Charita)

Left *Obverse Military Decoration - First
Class - Long Service (BE.D024)* (Spink &
Son Ltd)

wreath of laurel leaves which surround a dark blue pad, on to which is worked a 'W' which represents 'WAARNEMER', which translates as 'Observer'. The width of the badge, including the backing, is 91 mm and the height 52 mm. The measurements without the backing are respectively, 82 mm wingtip to wingtip and 43 mm from the base of the wreath to the top of the circle.

This badge was worn on the left breast above the tunic pocket and any service ribbons.

Army Air Service Pilot Observers' Wings [Cloth] (NE.A003) (A. Forman)

NE.A004 Army Air Service Pilot Observers' Wings (Metal) — 1940

This badge was introduced in 1940 and was made both in Holland and in Great Britain. It comprises a design that incorporates the Pilots' Badge (NE.A002), with a wreath of laurel leaves beneath. The outer leaves of the wreath on either side are cut out, giving a rough edge, while the inner rows are tight together giving a smooth appearance. There are six leaves in the inner and five in the outer row, joined together by a bow

Army Air Service Pilot Observers' Wings [Metal] (NE.A004) (A. Forman)

at the base. Each leaf has a raised central vein and a raised edge. In the centre of the wreath is a 'W', which is plain. The field is enamelled with opaque dark blue enamel. The badge measures 86 mm wingtip to wingtip and its height is 43 mm from the base of the wreath to the top of the circle.

The reverse is flat and may have no maker's mark or logo or can be found with the maker's mark or logo in two lines, as in the case of the Pilots' Badge (NE.A002). The badge was retained on the tunic by two round eyelets, through which passed a double piece of wire, like that used to secure a British cap badge. This is typical of the securing method found on Dutch and Belgian badges. The overall colour of the metal parts of the badge is gilt with a matt finish.

This badge was worn on the left breast above the tunic pocket and any service ribbons.

NE.A005 Army Air Service Observers' Wings (Cloth) — 14 October 1919

This badge was introduced on 14 October 1919 and comprises a design executed in gold bullion wire of a pair of wings which join to a circle at their centre. The circle consists of an outline of twisted gold bullion wire, with a central padded, dark blue field on to which is embroidered a capital 'W' for 'WAARNEMER', or 'Observer'. From the top line of fletching, which stretches from the wingtip to the circle, on either side running round the lower portion of the circle is a row of fifteen single feathers. There are four more lines of single feathers, running

Army Air Service Observers' Wings [Cloth] (NE.A005)

parallel from the junction on either side. From these protrude six lines of horizontal fletching, each with a slightly shorter length to the one directly above, thus forming a gentle inward sloping wingtip. This badge was worn on the left breast above the tunic pocket and any service ribbons.

NE.A006 Army Air Service Observers' Wings (Metal) — 1940

This badge was produced in both Holland and Great Britain and was introduced in 1940. It was constructed of metal, which was usually silver, and comprises a design incorporating a pair of wings which join to a circle. The circle's field is blue enamel and has a plain capital 'W'. The wings are formed of a continuous top line of fletching. Two lines of single feathers run from the circle beneath, six in the top row and four beneath. From these run five horizontal rows of fletching, each slightly shorter than that above. In this case, they are staggered

Army Air Service Observers' Wings [Metal] (NE.A006) (A. Forman)

backwards in a more pronounced way, in the form of small steps. The badge measures 90 mm wingtip to wingtip and the circle's height is 24 mm. The reverse is plain except for, in some cases, the maker's mark or logo with a large pin, similar to that found on the Pilots' Badge (NE.A002). This award was worn on the left

breast above the tunic pocket and any service ribbons.

Dutch Naval Air Service Wings
NE.N001 Naval Air Service Pilots' Wings (Cloth)

Naval pilots were awarded, on completion of their training, the same badge as that of the Army Air Service pilots (NE.A001). However, there are subtle differences in the design, namely in the position of the body of the eagle. If, however, this was intentional or purely a case of different manufacturers supplying the Navy, is not known to the author. I would personally take the stance that the difference in design was intentional. In this example the wing formation gives a defined neck to the eagle, as opposed to one where the neck is part

Naval Air Service Pilots' Wings [Cloth] (NE.N001)

of the two wings, as is the case in the Army pilots' badge. The two wings are of the same dimensions as the Army counterpart. It was worn on the left breast, above the tunic pocket and any service ribbons.

NE.N002 Naval Air Service Pilots' Wings (Metal) — 1940

This badge was produced from 1940 onwards and comprised an eagle in flight of the same general design as NE.A002. However, in this case the badge is double struck, that is to say with a male and female die, and constructed in lightweight silver. This gives the badge a more three-dimensional appearance than its counterpart.

The eagle in this badge is less stylized and comprises a pair of wings

joined to a distinct body, with the head looking downwards and, in this case, below the line of the lower edge of the wing. The beak just touches the circle upon which the eagle is superimposed. The circle is bordered by a plain raised edge and the field is of stippled translucent orange enamel and has the effect of being speckled. The relative position of the eagle on the circle is higher than that of the Army version.

The upper fletching stands proud of the rest of the wing configuration, which comprises two lines of single feathers running diagonally upwards from the eagle's body, along the line of the wing. There are six feathers on the upper and five on the lower of the bird's left wing and seven on the upper and six on the lower of the right wing. From these, on either side on each wing, are four lines of fletching, with semi-circular ends that are approximately 5 mm shorter than the corresponding ones above. Each feather or line of fletching has a raised central vein with the exception of the upper one that stands proud, which gives the illusion of diagonal irregular feathers, having a rope-like appearance. The width, wingtip to

Naval Air Service Pilots' Wings (NE.N002) (A. Forman)

wingtip, is 90 mm and the height of the circle is 25 mm. The reverse follows the design of the obverse, with a thin pin with hook and small hinge. The maker of this particular badge was TOYE and their name is found in an oblong box with silver stamped below. The badge was worn on the left breast above the tunic pocket and any service ribbons.

NE.N003 Naval Air Service Pilot Observers' Wings (Cloth) — 30 December 1930

This badge was introduced on 30 December 1930 and takes the same basic design as that of its Army counterpart (NE.A003). The eagle design is the same as that of the Naval Air Service pilot (NE.N001), with the embroidered wreath and 'W' for 'WAARNEMER' or 'Observer'. It was worn on the left breast above the tunic pocket and any service ribbons.

NE.N004 Naval Air Service Pilot Observers' Wings (Metal) — 1940

This badge was introduced in 1940 and was produced both in Holland and Great Britain. It takes the basic design of its Army counterpart (NE.A004), with the same designed eagle as that found in the Naval Air

Service Pilots' Wings (NE.N002) but the addition beneath of the wreath with the capital 'W' for 'WAARNE-MER'. The reverse is either plain or takes the obverse design, as in the case of the other double-struck badges. The maker's name is sometimes found, this usually being

TOYE. It would normally be accompanied by the silver mark which is 'Sterling' in words. The badge could have either two eyelets through which to put a retaining bar, or a thin needle pin. It was worn on the left breast above the tunic pocket and any service ribbons.

NE.N005 Naval Air Service Observers' Wings (Cloth) — 14 October 1919

This badge was introduced on 14 October 1919 and was similar to that of the Army Air Service Observer (NE.A005). It comprises a pair of wings with a gently curved upper line of fletching, which joins to a central circle outlined with a single wire line. The field is of navy blue with a large capital embroidered 'W' for 'WAARNEMER'. From the circle

extend three lines of individual feathers, four in each line. Beneath the top line of fletching are four lines of further fletching which are each slightly shorter than the one above, giving a gently sloping wingtip. The badge was worn on the left breast above the tunic pocket and any service ribbons.

NE.N006 Naval Air Service Observers' Wings (Metal) — 1940

This badge was introduced in 1940 and was produced in Britain. It comprises a pair of wings but, in this case, the wings surmount the circle and join the capital 'W' for 'WAAR-NEMER'. The 'W' has a raised outline, and the field has diagonal lines running downwards right to left. The design of the wings is identical to that of the Naval Air Service pilot (NE.N002), save for the angle that the top line of fletching produces at the junction of the 'W' in respect to that of the wings and the body of the

eagle. The field of the circle upon which the 'W' rests is of a pale blue opaque enamel. The outer line is plain.

The reverse has a needle pin and the maker's mark, 'TOYE', in a square and the word 'silver' beneath it. The overall colour of the exposed metal of the badge is gilt. The badge is of the double-struck or pressed-out variety. It was worn on the left breast above the tunic pocket and any service ribbons.

NE.N007 Naval Air Service Air Gunners' Wing (Cloth)

This badge comprises a circle with a single wing joined to its left, the viewer's right. It was produced in gold bullion embroidered on to a black backing. The circle is produced by a twisted line of bullion with a finer outer line. The central field is of blue melton which is slightly padded, on to which is embroidered, in capital letters, 'MS', which stand for 'MITRAILLEUR SCHUTTER', which translates as 'Air Gunner'. The wing is made up of a short upper line of fletching, which has a top line of embroidery that matches that which makes up the circle. The fletching is picked out below by a line of cotton stitching. Beneath this are three rows of individual single feathers, four in the top row, five in the middle and seven in the lower. These are pro-duced by semi-circular bullion embroidery and filled with flecked bullion wire. From these rows of feathers run four rows of fletching, which slope gently upwards. The stitching runs diagonally from upper right to lower left in the top row and

Naval Air Service Air Gunners' Wing [Cloth] (NE.N007) (A. Forman)

alternates in the descending rows. Each row is separated by a line of bullion wire and is progressively shorter. Thus, in the top line, there are fourteen lines of bullion, the next has ten, followed by eight and lastly six. The badge measures 66 mm with the backing and 56 mm circle to wingtip. The circle measures 22 mm high. The badge was worn on the left breast above the tunic pocket and any service ribbons.

NE.N008 Naval Air Service Air Gunners' Wing (Metal)

This badge comprises a circle with a single wing joined to its left, the viewer's right. It was produced in gilded silver. The circle, in this case, is

bordered by a ropelike outline and the field produced is enamelled in an opaque light blue. On to this field, let in again in a ropelike thin line, are the capital letters 'MS' which stand for 'MITRAILLEUR SCHUTTER' or 'Air Gunner'. The wing is applied separately, that is to say that the badge is produced in two parts which are then soldered together. The wing, in fact, is die struck and is used in the construction of the following badges, NE.N010 and NE.N012.

It comprises a bold upper plain line of fletching, which stops after 23 mm. Beneath this is a fan of single feathers in five rows. The top row has three, the next five, the next six, the next nine and the last ten. The last row is slightly longer than the preceding four and the feathers have a central vein and lines emanating from each side of it. From this fan emanate a further five lines of fletching, the top line having a bold upper line, each line beneath being slightly shorter than its predecessor, in fact by approximately 5 mm. Each line of fletching has diagonal lines running from upper right to lower left.

Naval Air Service Air Gunners' Wing [Metal] (NE.N008) (A. Forman)

The reverse is usually plain, that is to say on the circle where the silver mark can usually be found, but this does not hold true for every example encountered. The wing section has the outline of the obverse design being die struck or double-struck. There is a hinge soldered to the circle, through which is placed a wire pin. This is held in place by a catch in the form of a 'C' which is situated on the wingtip. The badge was worn on the left breast above the tunic pocket and any service ribbons.

NE.N009 Naval Air Service Air Telegraphist-Gunners' Wing (Cloth)

This badge comprises a circle with a single wing joined to its left, the viewer's right. It was produced in gold bullion embroidered on to a black backing. The circle is produced by a twisted line of bullion that has a finer outer line. The central field is of blue melton which is slightly padded, on to which is embroidered in capital letters, 'T' over 'MS', for 'TELE-PHONIEST-MITRAILLEUR

Naval Air Service Air Telegraphist Gunners' Wing [Cloth] (NE.N009)

SCHUTTER', which translates as 'Air Telegraphist-Gunner'. The wing is made up of a short upper line of fletching, which has a top line of embroidery that matches that which makes up the circle. The fletching is picked out below by a line of cotton stitching. Beneath this are three rows of individual single feathers, four in the top row, five in the middle and seven in the lower. These are produced by semi-circular bullion embroidery and filled with a flecked bullion wire. From these rows of feathers run four rows of fletching, which slope gently upwards. The stitching runs diagonally from upper right to lower left in the top row and alternates in the descending rows. Each row is separated by a line of bullion wire and is progressively shorter. Thus, in the top line, there are fourteen lines of bullion, the next has ten, followed by eight and lastly six. The badge measures 66 mm with the backing and 56 mm circle to wingtip. The circle measures 33 mm high. The badge was worn on the left breast above the tunic pocket and any service ribbons.

NE.N010 Naval Air Service Air Telegraphist-Gunners' Wing (Metal)

This badge again comprises a circle with single wing joined to its left, the viewer's right. It was produced in gilded silver. The circle, in this case, is bordered by a ropelike outline and the field produced is enamelled in an opaque light blue. On to this field, let in again in a ropelike thin line, are the capital letters 'T' over 'MS' standing for 'TELEPHONIEST-MITRAILL-EUR SCHUTTER', or 'Air Telegraphist-Gunner'. The wing is applied separately as on NE.N008 and NE.N012, and is identical to that described in NE.N008. The badge was worn on the left breast above the tunic pocket and any service ribbons.

NE.N011 Naval Air Service Air Telegraphists' Wing (Cloth)

This badge comprises a circle with a single wing joined to its left, the viewer's right. It was produced in gold bullion embroidered on to a black backing. The circle is produced by a twisted line of bullion that has a finer outer line. The central field is of blue melton which is slightly padded, on to which is embroidered a capital letter 'T', which stands for 'TELE-PHONIEST' or 'Air Telegraphist'. The wing is made up of a short upper line of fletching, which has a top line of embroidery that matches that which makes up the circle. The fletching is picked out below by a line of cotton stitching. Beneath this are three rows of individual single feathers, four in the top row, five in the middle and seven in the lower. These are produced by semi-circular bullion embroidery and filled with a flecked bullion wire. From these rows of feathers run four rows of fletching, which slope gently upwards. The stitching runs diagonally from upper right to lower left in the top row and alternates in the descending rows. Each row is separated by a line of bullion wire and is progressively shorter. Thus, in the top line, there are fourteen lines of bullion, the next has ten, followed by eight and lastly six. The badge measures 66 mm with the backing and 56 mm circle to wingtip. The circle measures 33 mm high. The badge was worn on the left breast above the tunic pocket and any service ribbons.

NE.N012 Naval Air Service Air Telegraphists' Wing (Metal)

This badge comprises a circle with single wing joined to its left, the viewer's right. It was produced in gilded silver. The circle, in this case, is bordered by a ropelike outline and the field produced is enamelled in an opaque light blue. On to this field, let in again in a ropelike thin line, is the capital letter 'T' for 'TELEPHONI-EST', or 'Air Telegraphist'. The wing is identical to that described under NE.N008. The badge was worn on

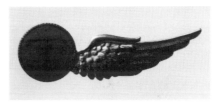

Naval Air Service Air Telegraphists Wing [Metal] (NE.N012) (A. Forman)

the left breast above the tunic pocket and any service ribbons.

Awards of the Norwegian armed forces

The defeat of Norway led to the Norwegian Army High Command arriving in England in July 1940. They began to draw up a 'military agreement' between themselves and the British government. By the time the fighting in Norway came to an end about 120 airmen and three aircraft had reached Britain. In 1940 training facilities were set up at Toronto in Canada. This camp, which became known as 'Little Norway', subsequently trained thousands of Norwegians who had come from the four corners of the globe. From 1941 the building of the Royal Norwegian Air Force was undertaken and this officially took place in August 1944 with the amalgamation of the Norwegian Army and Naval air services, which produced three squadrons, 330, 331 and 332 comprising approximately 200 officers and 1,400 other ranks serving with the RAF. This had been expanded by January 1945 to five squadrons operating eighty aircraft, with 483 officers and 2,099 other ranks. From August 1944, it became an independent force.

The Norwegian Navy managed to get two old destroyers, one submarine, ten fishing protection vessels and an assortment of other craft into British ports. The rebuilding process took place and this had been expanded to 58 assorted ships and 7,366 officers and ratings by the end of the war.

The Norwegian Army at the end of 1940 comprised 110 officers and 1,090 other ranks. When liberation came on 13 May 1945, it numbered approximately 2,500 men, who were mainly attached to British formations and headquarters staff. Their contribution to the war effort in an operational sense, due to their small numbers, was severely limited. The Resistance groups carried out daring and heroic actions, rendering much valuable assistance to the war effort.

Index to Norwegian Awards

Norwegian Air Force badges

Norwegian Naval Air Service badges

British awards to Norwegian nationals

	Medal	1st Bar	2nd Bar
GB.D006 The Distinguished Service Cross	62	3	1
GB.D007 The Distinguished Service Medal	41	1	

	Medal	1st Bar	2nd Bar
GB.D008 The Conspicuous Gallantry Medal(RN)	2		
GB.D009 Military Cross	19	3	
GB.D010 Military Medal	23		
GB.D001 The Distinguished Conduct Medal	9		
GB.D012 The Distinguished Flying Cross	80	13	1
GB.D013 The Air Force Cross	4		
GB.D015 The Distinguished Flying Medal	6		
GB.D016 The Air Force Medal	1		

NW.D001 The Order of St Olaf — Grand Cross
NW.D002 The Order of St Olaf — Commander with Star
NW.D003 The Order of St Olaf — Commander
NW.D004 The Order of St Olaf — Knights First Class
NW.D005 The Order of St Olaf — Knights

The Order of St Olaf was instituted on 21 August 1847 by King Oscar I and in the period of the Second World War comprised five classes which could be awarded for either outstanding civil or military service. In the case of the latter, crossed swords were added to the award, between the crown and the cross.

As this award was not intended primarily to reward Norwegian military personnel but was a more political award, I have included it in this work but have given it only a brief description, so that if the collector encounters it, he will be aware of its pedigree.

Obverse The Order of St Olaf - Grand Cross Breast Star (NW.D001) (Spink & Son Ltd)

The cross is of the Maltese type with ball finials. The edges of the arms are chamfered. The centre comprises a button or boss which has a line forming the outer edge. Within this is a second line, approximately twice its thickness. The central field that this line produces has superimposed on it a rampant Norwegian lion, holding an axe in its paw. The two lines are enamelled white, while the 'tramline' thus produced is enamelled blue and the central field is of red.

The arms of the cross are enamelled white, and between them are crowned 'O's, being the cypher of the founder, King Oscar I. From the upper 'V' of the cross is a segmented crown. The rim or brow of the crown has a design of ovals and diamonds, three and two respectively. The top of the crown has blobs of enamel to represent pearls and from the top, situated behind the orb and cross, is a crowned rampant Norwegian lion holding the Viking axe. The reverse is the same save that the central boss or medallion has an inscription, 'RET OG SANDHET', which translates as 'Justice and Truth'.

The overall metal colour of the classes is gold, except for the fifth class, which is silver. The ribbon colour for the relative ribbons is red with narrow white, blue and white edges, which represent the national colours of Norway.

I have not attempted to break down the individual types of insignia to the Order, the Order being in itself nearly the subject of a reference book. For example, on special occasions the award can be rendered with the addition of diamonds and as with all

Reverse The Order of St Olaf – Grand Cross Breast Star (NW.D001) (Spink & Son Ltd)

Obverse The Order of St Olaf – Grand Cross Sash Badge (NW.D001) (Spink & Son Ltd)

decorations that encompass the addition of diamonds, individual manufacturing techniques employed by jewellers, even in a short period, can create multifarious differences. The Grand Crosses also came with neck-chains or collars and these could be awarded, as with the diamonds, to varying grades. I hope the collector will allow this piece of licence of not attempting to give individual reference numbers but giving numbers for only the main types.

Reverse The Order of St Olaf – Grand Cross Sash Badge (NW.D001) (Spink & Son Ltd)

NW.D006 War Cross — 21 May 1941

On 7 June 1940 the King and his government were taken to Great Britain on board a British destroyer. For the majority of the Norwegian people, they remained the only legitimate government. General Otto Ruge, the Norwegian Commander in Chief, signed a capitulation order with the Germans on 10 June 1940, thus bringing the fighting in Norway to an end. The campaign had lasted for 62 days. The commander of the German Army Group Narvik, Generaloberst Edvard Dietl, once related to Hauptmann Uebe that, when he was awarded the Oak Leaves to the Knights Cross of the Iron Cross (D.019) for his exploits at Narvik, he reflected, 'I'm the hero of Narvik', the

title placed upon him by the German media. Then he said, 'Had the British stayed two more hours I would have left'. However, the fight was to be continued from London where Norwegians who escaped joined the various units that were subsequently set up.

To reward officers and men of these forces and their Allies, Norwegians or Allied subjects who rendered meritorious military or civil deeds, which aided in the defence of Norway, as well as members of her Merchant Marine, a Cross was introduced on 21 May 1941 which was produced in antiqued or patinated bronze. It comprises a straight-armed cross with club finials in the form of clover leaves at each end of the arms. The edges have slight recesses. The centre of the cross comprises a shield with flat top and gently curving pointed base. Round this runs another recessed line. Thus, a raised field is produced on which is a rampant Norwegian lion, holding an axe in its paw. Above the shield is the crown of Norway.

From the top of the cross is a suspension ball that has two lines to match the recesses on the arms of the cross, through which runs the ribbon suspender, which is thus hinged. It is formed as an upside-down stirrup and comprises a series of oak leaves punctuated with acorns. Across the top is a bar that runs beneath another,

thus a 'tramline' is formed which has the ribbon running through it.

The criterion for the award is that it should be bestowed upon the recipient for most conspicuous bravery and leadership before the enemy on land, at sea or in the air. Should the award be rendered again, it is denoted by the addition of a small bronze sword which is appended to the ribbon. The Cross could be awarded posthumously if necessary for the first or subsequent awards.

The ribbon can be found in two widths, 32 mm and 40 mm and in both cases is an overall red colour with a narrow blue centre stripe, flanked on either side by a narrow white stripe.

NW.D007 War Medal — 21 May 1941

This Medal was instituted on 21 May 1941 and comprises a round medal which has a slight edge rim. The obverse design comprises a head of King Haakon looking to the right, the viewer's left. It has a legend which runs round the bottom of the obverse of the medal, which is, 'ALT FOR NORGE', which translates as 'All for Norway'. This is started and stopped by a six-pointed star. Surrounding the top of the medal is the King's title, 'HAAKON VII'. These and the inscription are in capital letters.

The reverse design has, at its top, the inscription 'KRIGS MEDALJE', which translates as 'War Medal', with the royal cypher HVII entwined at each side, surmounted by the royal

Obverse War Medal (NW.D007) (Spink & Son Ltd)

crest, while at the base are crossed sprays of oak leaves.

At the top of the medal, as with the War Cross (NW.D006) is a ball suspender, through which runs a similar oak leaf stirrup but in this case, there is not the under retaining bar that produced the tramline for the ribbon to run through on NW.D006.

The Medal was to reward officers and men of the Norwegian and Allied fighting forces, as well as Norwegian and Allied civilians, who had meritoriously participated in the war on Norway's behalf, or rendered services

to the defence of that nation. The Medal, like the Cross, could be awarded posthumously and for subsequent awards, a Star could be awarded to represent that second or further award, a maximum of up to three Stars being allowed to be worn, appended to the ribbon.

The ribbon is red, 32 mm in width, with two yellow stripes 1.5 mm apart. The inner yellow on either side of the ribbon is inset from the edge by 1.5 mm and is 2 mm wide, while the next yellow on either side is almost 4 mm wide.

NW.D008 King Haakon VII Freedom Cross — 18 March 1945

This Cross was introduced on 18 March 1945 and is also referred to as King Haakon VII Cross of Liberty. The obverse design comprises a cross with gently sloping arms that run toward the centre which has, at that point, a boss or medallion with a raised edge. The centre thus produced is enamelled red in transparent enamel, on to which is placed the cypher HVII, for Haakon VII, which surmounts a 'V'. This is to represent victory. Above this central boss is the royal crown, the segments between the arches of the crown also being in a similar red enamel.

The cross ends have 'V's as their ends and an outline. The body of the cross is in opaque white enamel. From the upper cross arm's 'V' is positioned a box suspender, through which is fitted a bar which runs

Obverse King Haakon VII Freedom Cross (NW.D008) (Josef Charita)

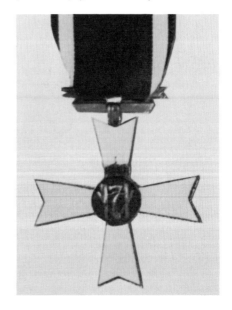

straight across, then forms a 'Z' shape at each end, the left-hand one being a mirror image of the other. The ends are then cut into a 'V' shape. The upper edge of this unusual suspender is recessed by approximately 1 mm.

The reverse is similar but the medallion has been removed and has the inscription across the horizontal arms of the cross, 'ALT FOR NORGE', which translates as 'All for Norway', with '7 JUNI' above and '1945' below it. The overall colour of the medal, on both obverse and reverse, is gold.

This Cross was to reward Norwe-gians and Allied service personnel who had rendered outstanding services during the war and could also be awarded to civilians, both Norwegian and foreign, for outstanding civil service to the Norwegian cause in time of war. There was no provision for this Cross to be awarded posthumously.

The ribbon is dark blue, 32 mm in width, with two stripes inset by 1.5 mm of white, which measure 4 mm. When the ribbon is only worn in its undress form, a gilt cypher 'H7' is applied to it.

NW.D009 King Haakon VII Freedom Medal — 18 March 1945

Obverse King Haakon VII Freedom Medal (NW.D009) (Spink & Son Ltd)

This Medal was instituted on 18 March 1945 and was also alluded to as the King Haakon VII Liberty Medal. It comprises a round medal produced in bronze that is antiqued or patinated. The obverse design comprises a circle of 82 dots set in approximately 4 mm. The 'tramline' that this produces with the outer edge, has the legend, 'ALT FOR NORGE', or 'All for Norway'. The beginning and end of the inscription are marked with a cross, beneath which are the dates 1940-1945. The central field has the royal cypher 'H7' that is superimposed on to a 'V', the 'V' emblematically representing victory. Above this is a flat-topped crown. From the top of the medal is a ball suspender which has a similar bar to that of the Cross, which runs straight across then forms a 'Z' shape at each end, the left-hand one being a mirror image of the other. The upper edge of this unusual suspender is recessed in by approximately by 1 mm. The ends of the bar are then cut into a 'V' shape.

This Medal was to reward Norwegian and Allied Service personnel who had rendered outstanding service during the war and was also awarded to civilians, both Norwegian and foreign, for outstanding civil service to the Norwegian cause in time of war. There is provision for the medal to be awarded posthumously.

The ribbon is plain dark blue, and 32 mm wide. When the ribbon is worn alone in the undress version, it has a bronze royal cypher comprising 'H7' surmounted by a crown.

NW.D010 Participation Medal 1940-1945 — 1945

This award comprises a round medal that has, as its obverse design, an inner line approximately inset by 4 mm. On to this is the date 9 April 1940, which is followed underneath by the date 8 Mai 1945. These two dates are separated by four pellets arranged in a diamond fashion design. To the inner line are eight semi-circles or arches, the field thus formed being crosshatched diagonally and each chequer being filled with a diamond. On to this field is set a flat-topped shield with pointed base, on to which is a crowned rampant lion of Norway, holding an axe in its paw. The shield is surmounted by a royal crown.

The intention of this medal was to reward those members of the underground movement who had been involved both at home and abroad and had served valiantly in that service.

The medal had an integral suspension ball through which was placed

Obverse Participation Medal 1940-1945 (NW.D010) (Spink & Son Ltd)

the ribbon ring. Through this was positioned a 32 mm white ribbon which has an edge stripe 8 mm wide on either side, with two stripes of blue 2 mm wide and set 8 mm apart.

NW.D011 King Haakon VII 70th Anniversary Medal — 3 August 1942

This Medal was introduced on 3 August 1942 to commemorate King Haakon's 70th birthday. It was constructed of bronze and consists of an obverse design that has an effigy of the King in military uniform. There is an inscription that runs around the rim, 'HAAKON 7 NORGES KONGE', which translates as 'Haakon 7 King of Norway'. The medal is surmounted by a crown, through which the ribbon is positioned.

The medal was awarded to all Norwegian personnel who were serving in any of the volunteer units that were stationed in Great Britain or the Danish colonies. This medal was used as propaganda and a morale booster for those troops, as little to encourage them was occurring either in the German theatre of operations that this book covers, or the Japanese theatre. Thus the King's 70th birthday became a valuable rallying point.

The ribbon is red and 33 mm wide, with two yellow centre stripes measuring 3 mm which are set 3 mm apart.

Norwegian Air Force Badges
NW.A001 Air Force Pilots' Badge — 1934

This badge was instituted in February 1926 in its first form and comprised an embroidered badge produced on a cloth backing, which was red until 1934 when the background was changed to green. It comprises a pair of wings which have a continuous top line of fletching. It has a small scallop in each wing and a larger central one, above which is found a shield with the rampant lion of Norway holding an axe in its paws. This is in an open topped wreath. Surmounting the shield and placed between the arms of the wreath, is the crown of Norway with five arches. The segments between the arches are filled in with horizontal lines of embroidery. The central scallop has two rows of 'V'-shaped pin feathers pointing downwards, eight in the top row and seven in the second. Beneath this are three

Air Force Pilots' Badge (NW.A001)

larger feathers, once more pointing downwards, that give the impression of a bird's tail. Beneath this and the upper line on either side, are five lines of fletching. The stitching is formed diagonally and points outwards in each direction. The individual wing fletch is then picked out in silver wire. The overall colour of the embroidery of the badge is of silver bullion thread. The badge was worn on the right breast pocket of the tunic.

NW.A002 Air Force Observers' Badge — 1934

Air Force Observers' Badge (NW.A002)

This badge was also instituted in February 1926 and originally embroidered on to a red background, but it was redesigned in 1934 and placed on a green background. The new badge comprises a half wing pointing to the right, the viewer's left, and was worn on the right breast pocket of the tunic.

The central design of this badge comprises a shield with the rampant lion of Norway holding an axe in its paw. This is surmounted by a five-arched crown. The segments between the arches are again filled in with horizontal lines of embroidery.

The wing in this badge is subtly different to those of the preceding design NW.A001, in as much that the top line of the wing slopes downwards and then follows the line of the shield to its bottom. From this line are two rows of chequerboard squares, from which emanate four more rows of fletching. The stitching in these is vertical. The overall colour of the badge is silver, deriving from its construction out of silver bullion. The badge was worn on the right breast pocket of the tunic.

NW.A003 Air Force Pilots' Badge — after 11 June 1940

This badge was produced in either Britain or Canada and was to reward pilots of the newly-created free Norwegian Air Force. Whether this badge replaced the first type is a little in doubt, as it is highly possible that both were worn together, that is to say pilots who had their original version, NW.A001, continued to wear it until another was required, while newly-qualified pilots were issued with the new design.

The design of the badge is very similar to the former badge, NW.A001, save for the fact that the segments between the arches of the crown and the field of the shield are produced by the addition of a red underlay. The silver bullion work is embroidered on to a blue-grey underlay of the same general colour used

Air Force Pilots' Badge (NW.A003)

for the wings of the RAF. I would refer the reader to the description in NW. A001. The badge was worn on the right breast of the tunic.

NW.A004 Air Force Observers' Badge — after 11 June 1940

This badge took a totally new design from its previous counterpart, NW.A002, in the fact that it now comprised two wings emanating from an oval. The design is embroidered on to a blue-grey underlay of the same general colour used for the wings of the RAF in silver bullion. The wing design is of a downward beat shape, that is to say the upper line of fletching runs from wingtip to wingtip, the tips being below the line of the upper edge. This upper edge rises, then falls in the centre, forming a 'V' shape. Below this 'V' the oval is positioned. In the 'V' produced at the joint of the wings (that is, above the oval) are positioned the shield and royal crown. The underlay of this part of the design is in red. Thus the field of the shield is red with the rampant Norwegian lion holding an axe in its

paws, while the segments between the arches of the crown are picked out in red. Within the oval, on a blue-grey field, is a stylized 'S'.

Each wing comprises four lines of fletching that emanate from the oval and follow the line of the upper row but are proportionately reduced in length. The badge was worn on the right breast of the tunic.

Air Force Observers' Badge (NW.A004)

NW.A005 Air Force Wireless Operator Air Gunners' Badge — 1944

During the period between 10 June 1940 and the end of the war, it became apparent that air crew members required varying qualification badges to indicate their branch of service. This practice was followed by the Norwegians who introduced this badge in conformity to those of the British RAF and it is therefore possible that this badge was introduced in 1944 at the same time as the British counterpart, GB.A010.

The design of the badge takes the form of a pair of wings which, in this case, emanate from a circle. The badge is executed in silver bullion on a blue-grey background or underlay of the same general colour that was used for the wings of the RAF. The shield and crown arch segments are exposed in red. The shield has the Norwegian rampant lion holding an axe in its paw. The shield and crown are positioned above the wing in its 'V' and directly above the circle. In this case, the shield and circle in fact touch at this point and become the

Air Force Wireless Operator Air Gunners' Badge (NW.A005)

fulcrum of the axis of the wing. Beneath this wing are three lines of wavy fletching, on either side of the circle and emanating from it. These lines are to represent the radio waves or 'sparks' of a radio operator. The circle is divided at an angle of 45 degrees and produces two fields which have, in the upper segment, a capital 'R' and in the lower segment, a capital 'S'. Both letters are slightly slanted in a degree that follows the central bisecting line. The badge was worn on the right breast of the tunic.

NW.A006 Air Force Flight Engineer and Air Gunners' Badge — 1944

This is of similar design to NW.A005 except that each line of fletching follows the top line, as opposed to the sparked type in the former badge.

The circle has the letters M/S in the same manner. The badge was worn on the right breast of the tunic.

Air Force Flight Engineer and Air Gunners'
Badge (NW.A006)

NW.A007 Air Force Navigators' Badge — 10 June 1940

This badge was the same as the Pilots' Badge NW.A003 but with the tail feathers removed and a Circle substituted with a capital N placed within it. The badge was worn on the right breast of the tunic.

Air Force Navigators' Badge (NW.A007)

Norwegian Naval Air Service badges
NW.N001 Naval Air Service Pilots' Badge — 1934

This badge is identical to its Air Force counterpart, NW.A001, but in this case the underlay is navy blue and the badge is executed in gold bullion embroidery.

NW.N002 Naval Air Service Observers' Badge — 1934

This badge is identical to its Air Force counterpart, NW.A002, but in this case the underlay is navy blue and the badge is executed in gold bullion embroidery.

NW.N003 Naval Air Service Pilot's Badge — after 11 June 1940

This badge is identical to its Air Force counterpart, NW.A003, but in this case the underlay is navy blue and the badge is executed in gold bullion embroidery.

NW.N004 Naval Air Service Observers' Badge — after 11 June 1940

This badge is identical to its Air Force counterpart, NW.A004, but in this case the underlay is navy blue and the badge is executed in gold bullion embroidery.

NW.N005 Naval Air Service Wireless Operator Air Gunners' Badge — 1944

This badge is identical to its Air Force counterpart, NW. A005, but in this case the underlay is navy blue and the badge is executed in gold bullion embroidery.

NW.N006 Naval Air Service Flight Engineer and Air Gunners' Badge — 1944

This badge is identical to its Air Force counterpart NW.A006, but in this case the underlay is navy blue and the badge is executed in gold bullion embroidery.

NW.N007 Naval Air Service Navigators' Badge — 10 June 1940

This badge is identical to its Air Force counterpart NW.A007, but in this case the underlay is navy blue and the badge is executed in gold bullion embroidery.

Awards of the Danish armed forces

For the Germans, the occupation of Denmark went with Swiss watch precision. Denmark was seized before her citizens had time to appreciate what was happening, with the consequence that neither the King nor any member of his government had any chance to escape. The circumstances surrounding the invasion that occurred in the early dawn of 9 April 1940 meant that the Blitzkrieg which the Germans mounted met virtually no resistance. However, thirteen Danish soldiers were killed and 23 wounded which can be considered, in military terms, little more than a skirmish and thus before the Danes had had their breakfast, it was all over.

Of all the occupied countries Denmark held the title of being the most unusual, apart from France which had had an armistice, for Denmark was allowed to hold a general election. This took place on 23 March 1943 and nowhere else in occupied Europe was an appeal to a mass electorate permitted. Denmark was left free to choose a new government from whom they should please, except for Communists who were banned. The result changed nothing, but it produced the largest turnout in Danish polling history, 88.5 per cent. The major parties increased their share of the vote but only in relationship to the increase in the vote; however, Clausen's Nazi Party actually increased its share of the poll. Thus, the political conditions in Denmark made an outside fighting force less probable than in any other occupied territories, since there was no government in exile. Approximately only 905 Danes of both sexes found their way to Great Britain. A few selected officers were smuggled out to serve in special units and about twenty Danish naval officers found their way to England where they served in the Royal Navy. In 1943 a Danish unit was formed within the Royal Navy and by the end of the war a number of minesweepers had Danish crews. In May 1945, these ships arrived in Copenhagen, which was to be the basis of the new Danish Navy, together with a Danish flotilla that had been in Sweden. On the other hand, there were many thousands of Danes in the German armed forces. British intelligence reckoned that in 1942 there were 180 volunteers in the actual German labour service, (RAD). Danish volunteers also served in large numbers in the

Waffen-SS, the Speer Legion in Norway. Many of the Waffen-SS volunteers died at Stalingrad and it has been estimated that a total of 398 Danes gave their lives in the German service, while 78 died in the service of the Allies. The bravery and importance of the Resistance and the importance of the items and refugees they smuggled to Sweden, was greater than their numerical size.

Index to Danish Awards

Danish Flying Wings

British award to Danish nationals

DN.D001 King Christian X Medal for Participation in the War 1940-1945 — 3 May 1946

This Medal was instituted on 3 May 1946 and consists of a round silver medal surmounted by a crown. The obverse design has that of the head of the monarch facing to the right, which was executed by H. Salomon.

The medal is surrounded by the inscription 'CHRISTIAN X. MIN GUD. MIT LAND. MIN AERE.' which translates as 'Christian X My God. My country. My honour'. The reverse design comprises an inscription formed in five lines. In the first is 'FOR.DELTAGELSE.' then 'I ALLIERET. KRIGSTJENESTE.' and finally the date '1940-45', the translation of which is, 'For participation in the allied war service 1940-45'. There were 905 Danish men and women who served with the Allied forces, of whom 78 perished. These received the medal posthumously and this is the only case in which medals of that nation were so awarded.

From the crown is a ribbon suspender through which runs a 27 mm red ribbon furled in Danish style. The ribbon has a 14 mm central panel of white on which are three 1.5 mm stripes of red, spaced 2 mm apart.

DN.D002 King Christian X Medal in Commemoration of the Liberation — 5 May 1945

This Medal was instituted on 5 May 1945 and comprises a round silver medal 31 mm in diameter, surmounted by a crown. The obverse design has the head of the monarch facing to the right and was executed once again by H. Salomon. The medal is surrounded by an inscription, which reads in Latin, 'CHRISTIANUS X REX DANIAE', or 'Christian X King of Denmark'. The reverse design comprises an inscription formed in three lines, which is flanked by two oak branches, one either side, and tied at the base with a ribbon tie. The inscription is 'PRO' followed by 'DANIAE' and then the date '1940-45', which translates as 'For Denmark 1940-45'. This inscription gives rise to the Medal's other nomenclature of the Pro Daniae Medal or Medal of Liberty.

The Medal was to reward special services rendered to Denmark that were occasioned during the German occupation by both Danes and other nationals living outside Denmark and was conferred on 3,102 recipients.

From the crown is a ribbon suspender, through which runs a 27 mm red ribbon, furled in Danish style, and which has a white centre with a width of 11 mm.

Danish Flying Wings

DN.A001 Army Pilots' Badge — 27 February 1925-1951

This badge is constructed of gold bullion wire embroidered on to a black wool underlay or background. Its design was greatly influenced by that of British flying badges and comprises a pair of wings emanating from an oval. This is surmounted by the royal crown. The actual arms of the wings are downswept in a continuous curve. The top is outlined in a bold wire line. Beneath this is the main band of fletching which runs from the oval to form the upper tip. Into this run eight lines of fletching which have a pencil point to the lower edge. The embroidery lines on either wing run diagonally downwards towards the oval. The upper joint of the wing is picked out in black stitching, as is a line halfway beneath this first stitch line. The crown's cut-out

Army Pilots' Badge (DN.A001)

portions are picked out in red silk. The overall measurements of the wings are 36 mm vertically and 95 mm horizontally. The field of the central oval has a pair of crossed rifles surmounted by a canon barrel. This device is produced in metal and has a gilded finish. The badge was worn sewn on to the right breast of the uniform.

DN.A002 Army Observers' Badge — 1941–1951

This badge was introduced in 1941 and comprises a half set of wings executed in bullion and embroidered, in this case on a khaki instead of a black underlay. To all intents and purposes the badge is otherwise iden-

tical to the Pilots' Badge, DN.A001, the measurements however being 39 mm vertically and 59 mm horizontally. It was also worn on the right breast of the tunic.

Army Observers' Badge (DN.A002)

DN.N001 Naval Pilots' Badge — 1923

This badge is similar in configuration to that of the Army Pilots' Badge (DN.A001), and as it was instituted two years before the Army version it would be a fair assumption to consider that the Army followed the senior service in its design. However, this badge is slightly smaller, being only 86 mm in length, but slightly higher, measuring 39 mm vertically. The crown has the addition of green to the red of the army badge. The most fundamental difference is the addition of the fouled anchor, which are placed in the central oval. This

Naval Pilots' Badge (DN.N001)

badge was awarded to pilot captains of flying boats of the Danish Navy and was worn sewn on to the right breast pocket of the tunic.

DN.N002 Naval Pilots' Badge (Metal) — 1923

This badge is identical to its embroidered counterpart, DN. N001, but is produced in gilded metal. It was worn pinned on to the right breast pocket of the tunic and recognized, as did its predecessor, pilot captains of flying boats of the Danish Navy.

Awards of the Belgian Forces

When war broke out in September 1939, Belgium remained neutral. On 10 May 1940 Germany, which had only three years previously guaranteed her inviolability, now struck her down without a warning or pretext in a severe campaign which lasted eighteen days. In the early hours of 28 May 1940, King Leopold III, without consulting or even informing his Allies, ordered the immediate capitulation of all the Belgian armed forces. His action was condemned as treachery by his Allies and was repudiated by his own government. The French were especially bitter. Prime Minister Paul Reynaud retorted that Leopold had little concern for the British and French soldiers who had responded to Leopold's anguished appeals to aid his stricken country. Leopold had instructed them to lay down their arms, an act unprecedented in history. As a result of these treacherous actions, the Prime Minister ordered his name to be removed from the roll of the Legion of Honour. However, the Vichy government later restored Leopold's name to the roll. (Such instances of medals being reviewed by the Vichy government have been explained in the chapter on France and because of these actions, certain medals of that regime have been included, which at first may seem an anomaly.)

The Belgian government withdrew to France where, at an emergency session in Limoges, it declared the capitulation order to be illegal and disassociated itself entirely from it, thus leaving the way clear for a government in exile. The Belgian government made its way to London and was recognized by most of the nations of the free world. It succeeded in rallying the bulk of the Belgian merchant fleet as well as miscellaneous Army and Air Force units.

The German occupation set a legal situation that was a little more complex under international law, since before leaving the country in May 1940 the government had transferred their power to the Secretaries General. The King remained in Belgium, the nominal Head of State, but refused to exercise his duties. Hubert Pierlot, who headed the exiled government in London, was a prosaic, uninspiring person, one might have even called him dull. He did not inspire waverers to rally to the cause or fortify the resistance movement in Belgium.

From those who had escaped to Britain by various means it was learned that, due to uncertainty over the legal position, no systematic attempt had been made to evacuate the Belgian forces left by that treacherous order to lay down their arms. About 120 Belgian airmen reached England by various routes, in time to fight in the Battle of Britain. On 21 June Lieutenant-General van Strydonck began to form the few hundred Army personnel into two companies, one to be combat and the other non-combat. On 21 February 1942 the Belgian Air Force was reconstituted in Britain, with the overwhelming majority serving in the Belgian squadrons of the RAF, numbers 349 and 350. Thus the road back to the liberation of Belgium by her own troops had begun. The resistance in the country was to be strengthened. It was from these embryo units that the Free Belgian Forces were formed and it was to these units and for their courage, that the medals in this section were awarded.

Index to Belgian Awards

Above *Obverse Croix de Guerre 1940–1945 (BE.D028* (Spink & Son Ltd)

Above right *Obverse Escapers' Cross 1940–1945 (BE.D029)* (Josef Charita)

Right *Obverse War Medal 1940–1945 (BE.D030) with Crossed Swords emblem on ribbon*

Above left *Reverse Medal of the Resistance Army 1940–1945 (BE.D031)*

Above *Obverse Medal for Volunteers 1940–1945 (BE.D032)* (Spink & Son Ltd)

Left *Obverse Civil Decoration 1940–1945 First Class Cross (BE.D034)* (Josef Charita)

Above *Obverse Cross for Political Prisoners 1940-1945 (BE.D039)* (Josef Charita)

Above right *Reverse Medal for Prisoners of War 1940-1945 (BE.D040)*

Right *Obverse Medal for Refractories 1940-1945 (BE.D042)* (Josef Charita)

Above left *Reverse Medal of Belgian Grati-tude 1940-1945 Bronze (BE.D045)*(Josef Charita)

Above *Obverse African War Medal 1940-1945 (BE.D047)*

Left *Obverse Medal of the Military Fighters of the 1940-1945 War (BE.D048)* (Josef Charita)

Belgian Flying Wings

British awards to Belgian nationals

	Medal	1st Bar	2nd Bar
GB.D006 The Distinguished Service Cross	2		
GB.D009 Military Cross	35		
GB.D009 Military Medal	24		
GB.D011 The Distinguished Conduct Medal	11		
GB.D012 The Distinguished Flying Cross	59	5	1
GB.D013 The Air Force Cross	5		
GB.D015 The Distinguished Flying Medal	1		

Order of Leopold — 11 July 1832

This order was introduced by King Leopold I on 11 July 1832 to reward both Belgians and foreigners who had rendered services to Belgium. Initially it was awarded in four grades, but in 1839 this was extended to five. This reorganization had civil and military grades, the latter being indicated by the addition of crossed swords. In 1934 the addition of a naval version was introduced to the grading which replaced the swords for all grades awarded to naval personnel. The Order thus may be conferred upon officers for gallantry in the field and NCOs, other ranks and civilians for war service. Civilians thus decorated for service in the First World War were denoted by the addition of a gold or silver star to the ribbon of the 4th and 5th class of the Order, and also, according to service,

a centre stripe or broader stripes of gold to the ribbon which was introduced by royal decree on 26 June 1919. This decree covered the preferment of other national awards made to civilians for distinguished war service. However, the scope of this book is for those awards of the Second World War and I will describe the civilian versions that are applicable to the period 1940-1945; the military grades are identical but with the application of either swords or anchors denoting to which branch of service the recipient belonged. The reader has then only to superimpose either of the types on to the descriptions discussed during this chapter.

The Order of Leopold, founded by King Leopold 1 11 July 1832 Military Division (Kai Meyer collection).

BE.D001 Grand Cross — Breast Star — 11 July 1832
BE.D002 Grand Cross — Breast Star with Swords — 1839
BE.D003 Grand Cross — Breast Star with Anchors — 1934

The Breast Star comprises an eight-pointed starburst with the points at 12, 3, 6 and 9 o'clock relatively. These are slightly larger and longer in construction than those in the quadrants which are proportionately smaller.

The arms of all the rays are slightly convex and the obverse is of a cut or diamond faceted construction, similar to that found on marcasite. The central boss design comprises four portions, the outer one being a ring of fifty similar cut diamonds. Then there is a circle that has another inner but slightly thicker line. Between these two lines is found the legend, 'L'UNION FAIT LA FORCE', which translates as 'Unity Makes Strength'. However, it is important to point out that by royal decree on 24 October 1951, where the inscription was only found in French, from that date the inscription has to be in both French and Dutch. The use of the word 'Dutch' is of importance, considering Flemish national movements' involvement with the Germans in the two world wars. The fascist awards of those Flemish movements will be covered in the volume on German Foreign Volunteer units. Thus from 24 October 1951 the Flemish inscription, 'EENDRACHT MAAKT MACHT' was also employed beneath the French inscription. In the case of the French inscription there is a small six-pointed star with a laurel sprig on either side. The design is next accomplished by a repeat of the diamond cut circle. There is a subtle difference in these

Obverse The Order of Leopold Grand Cross – Breast Star with Swords (BE.D002) (Josef Charita)

two rows of diamond cuts. In the French-only legend type, they are smaller in both rows than those found in the dual-legend version. The field on to which the legend is applied is of red translucent enamel. The central circle is of black transparent enamel with a rampant, crowned, Belgian lion. The whole of the central boss is gilded or gold-plated. The reverse is fluted with a wide vertical pin.

BE.D004 Grand Cross Sash Badge — 11 July 1832
BE.D005 Grand Cross Sash Badge with Swords — 1839
BE.D006 Grand Cross — Sash Badge with Anchors — 1934

The Sash Badge comprises a Maltese Cross which has, at each point of the arms, a ball. The edges of the arms are slightly chamfered and these and the balls are gilded or gold-plated. The field thus created between the chamfered lines of the arms of the cross are of white opaque enamel, with a matching gold line running round the arm. The central boss design comprises four portions, the outer one being a ring of fifty similar cut diamonds. Then there is a circle that has another inner but slightly thicker line. Between these two lines is again found the legend, 'L' UNION FAIT LA FORCE'. Again, from 1951 the inscription has been in both French and Dutch. The 'V' formed below the lower arm of the cross has a bow tie for a laurel and oak wreath which runs round the right- and left-hand edge of the badge of the insignia. The leaves are in transparent green enamel and interspersed with red enamelled laurel berries, six in number on the right. The opposite side is made up of transparent green oak leaves. Above the upper arm is a crown of an open work design in a five-arched construction. It is below this crown that the crossed swords or anchors are found; the anchors are not crossed but placed top to top horizontally, pointing outwards. The 'T's of the anchor tops join together to make the top of the insignia and the hinge fulcrum of the crown. The Sash Badge, of whichever type, is found suspended from just beneath the bow of the sash and is usually clipped on to a small spring clip that allows for its easy removal.

The sash itself is a watered purple silk band which measures approximately 100 mm in width. The length of the sash can be tailored to the individual height of the recipient. It is worn over the right shoulder and falls to the left hip where the bow rests with two ends beneath, on which rests the Sash Badge of the Order.

BE.D007 Grand Cross — Metal Collar — 11 July 1832
BE.D008 Grand Cross — Metal Collar with Swords — 1839
BE.D009 Grand Cross — Metal Collar with Anchors — 1934

This is worn on special occasions and from this collar is suspended the Grand Cross Sash Badge, as previously described. The metal collar consists of a crown at the centre of the design which is flanked on either side by a rampant Belgian lion, both of which face inwards towards the crown. This is then followed by a script 'L R', which is the cypher for 'Leopold Rex'. The design is repeated and consists of, in all, nine royal crowns, seven 'L R' monograms and eighteen Belgian rampant lions. These are all connected together by a single strand, plain link chain which is attached at the top and bottom of the cyphers and the lions and the crowns. The Sash Badge is attached by three links, one either side of the central crown, running down to a larger ring that runs through the body of the orb that surmounts the five-arched open work crown.

BE.D010 Grand Officer — Breast Star — 11 July 1832
BE.D011 Grand Officer — Breast Star with Swords — 1839
BE.D012 Grand Officer — Breast Star with Anchors — 1934

The Star in this case comprises a Maltese Cross which has a raised edge running round the field. The field thus produced comprises a design made up of diamond facets similar to marcasite. The cross's points have balls applied to each of them. The quarters between each of the arms are made up of five rays. Each ray has a raised outer line. The whole of the star is convex and the centre has the obverse central design

Obverse The Order of Leopold - Grand Officer - Breast Star with Anchors (BE.D012) (Josef Charita)

which is featured throughout the whole of the series and comprises four portions, the outer one being a ring of fifty similar cut diamonds. Then there is a circle that has another inner but slightly thicker line. Between these two lines is found the legend, 'L'UNION FAIT LA FORCE', which since 1951 has been repeated in Dutch. The reverse is polished and has a massive vertical pin.

The swords or anchors are placed midway of the rays that make up the quarters of the cross and are in gilt. In the case of the swords, the hilts are downwards and in the case of the anchors the hooks are downwards.

BE.D013 Commander — 11 July 1832
BE.D014 Commander with Swords — 1839
BE.D015 Commander with Anchors — 1934

This badge is identical to that of the Grand Cross Sash Badge but is slightly smaller and consists of a white enamelled cross. The central boss design comprises four portions, the outer one being a ring of fifty similar cut diamonds. Then there is a circle that has another inner but slightly thicker line. Between these two lines is found the legend, 'L'UNION FAIT LA FORCE', repeated in Dutch since 1951. The Commander's Order is worn round the neck on a ribbon of purple watered silk.

Obverse The Order of Leopold - Commander - with Swords (BE.D014) (Josef Charita)

BE.D016 Officer — 11 July 1832
BE.D017 Officer with Swords — 1839
BE.D018 Officer with Anchors — 1934

This badge is identical to both the Grand Cross Sash Badge and Commander's Badge, but is smaller. The Officer's Badge in all three classes is worn from a watered purple ribbon on the chest which has a rosette applied upon it. The swords and anchors devices are applied beneath the crown in the relevant military or naval versions.

Left *Obverse The Order of Leopold - Officers - with Swords (BE.D017)* (Josef Charita)

Far left *Obverse The Order of Leopold - Officers - with Swords (BE.D017). Variation to the size of Swords* (Josef Charita)

BE.D019 Knight — 11 July 1832
BE.D020 Knight with Swords — 1839
BE.D021 Knight with Anchors — 1934

This badge is identical to the Grand Cross Sash Badge and Commander's Badge and is the same size as that of the Officer's, but in this case, the crown and the badge are all produced

Reverse The Order of Leopold - Knights - with Swords (BE.D020) (Josef Charita)

in silver. The body of the cross is of white enamel following the overall design of the series but only the central boss is gilt. It is also worn, as is the Officer's Badge, from a purple watered ribbon on the chest, but in this case it is plain and without the rosette. The swords and anchors are positioned beneath the crown in this order as well.

BE.D022 Military Cross — First Class — 11 February 1885
BE.D023 Military Cross — Second Class — 1895

This Medal was introduced on 11 February 1885 to reward officers for long service. This was subsequently changed by an order in 1895 and from then on was split into two grades. These basically took the same period of time, namely 25 years, but in the case of the First Class, was awarded to officers for 25 years' service as an officer and in the case of the Second Class for 25 years' military service, which was calculated from the commencement of the recipient's service in the Army or from when he had been a cadet at a military school. In special cases this decoration can also be conferred on non-Belgian nationals.

The two Crosses are of identical design, consisting of a Maltese Cross which has ball finials at each point. In the 'V' created in the upper arm is an inverted 'V' suspender which connects to an open work crown which comprises five arches. This 'V' suspender is pivoted and also has a raised edge. The arms of the cross also have a raised edge. There is a central boss which has a row of dots

and a convex field, on which is the lion of Belgium. All of these parts are

Obverse Military Cross First Class (BE.D022) (Josef Charita)

gilded. The field produced on the arms of the cross on both the obverse and reverse, is of opaque black enamel. Between the arms of the cross are a pair of crossed swords of the double-edged variety. These are also finished, that is to say the design is repeated on both sides, and are gilded. The reverse of the medal is identical to the obverse except that the central boss bears the relevant monarch's monogram. In the case of the medals covered in this section it is 'L' for Leopold. The crown has a ribbon ring through which runs the ribbon, which is made up of a thin green stripe, broad red, central green, broad red and thin green stripe. In the case of the First Class Medal a rosette is added to the ribbon to denote its grade. Both medals are worn on the chest.

Obverse Military Cross Second Class (BE.D023)(Josef Charita)

Reverse Military Cross Second Class (BE.D023) (Josef Charita)

BE.D024 Military Decoration — First Class — Long Service — 1902
BE.D025 Military Decoration — Second Class — Long Service — 1873
BE.D026 Military Decoration — First Class — Bravery — 1902
BE.D027 Military Decoration — Second Class — Bravery — 1873

This decoration was instituted in 1873 for long service and for acts of bravery. However, in 1900 a First Class decoration was added to the order of the award. This was then distinguished by a large gilt chevron.

This was again revised in 1902 and gave rise to the final grading which lasted until 1946 and 1952 when other fine tuning was introduced. These are outside the scope of this work, but will be covered in the

Reverse Military Decoration - First Class - Long Service (BE.D024) (Spink & Son Ltd)

volume on awards from 1945 to the present day. The 1902 reforms produced two divisions with a Cross in two classes, with and without chevrons applied to the ribbon. The First Class Cross is awarded to officers and non-commissioned officers, while the Second Class is for the rank and file.

The first division is for that of long service while the other is for bravery, self-sacrifice or special achievement. The Cross and the chevrons are identical and only the ribbons distinguish the awards from one another.

The cross is a George Cross with a central boss. The outer edge of the cross is raised and the field is lined horizontally. Likewise, the boss has a raised outer edge and then another raised inner line. The field created between these lines is plain and on to this is applied the legend, 'L'UNION FAIT LA FORCE' which translates as 'Unity Makes Strength'. There is a small five-pointed star between the beginning and the end of the legend, above the middle of the lower arm of the cross. The circle of the centre of the boss has a dotted field on to which is placed the lion of Belgium. Between the arms of the cross are four pencil pointed rays. Above the top arm is the Belgian royal crown which is constructed in a solid format. This has a ball or orb at its top through which runs the ribbon ring.

The reverse is identical without the legend on the central boss. The overall colour is of gilt as is that of the chevrons, which are constructed with a wide raised edge. This is polished and the field between those edges is pebbled.

The ribbon for long service is red with four groups of yellow, black and yellow stripes equally spaced, and for bravery is red with three 3 mm edged stripes of black on the inner, yellow and red on the outer. Those who have received the award and been Mentioned in Despatches in time of war, receive a silver palm leaf which, in the case of the 1940-1945 war, has an 'L' for Leopold monogram. This monogrammed palm is worn on the ribbon of the relevant grade or class.

BE.D028 Croix de Guerre 1940-1945 — 1941

The Belgian government in exile in Great Britain instituted on 20 July 1941 this Cross to reward the members of the Army, Navy and Air

Force for bravery in the face of the enemy. This medal could also be awarded to a unit as a unit citation and to non-Belgian nationals.

The design of the Cross is the same as that employed in the Croix de Guerre 1914-1918. It consists of a bronze Maltese Cross with ball finials at each tip of the arms. The edges of the cross are raised. The central boss has a raised edge then a row of dots or pellets. Into this is a Belgian lion. The field that comprises that of the arms of the cross is pebbled. Through the angles of the arms of the cross are crossed swords of the double-edged variety and these are finished on the reverse as well as the obverse. The upper arm has an inverted 'V' that joins the cross to an open work Belgian crown of five-arch design. Through the top of the crown, through the ball or orb, is fitted a ribbon ring.

The reverse is identical to the obverse save for the design of the boss that has, instead of the lion, the royal monogram 'L' for Leopold.

The ribbon is red with three 1 mm green stripes, inset 2 mm and 2 mm apart. Recipients who have been Mentioned in Despatches wear a bronze or silver lion, which indicates an Army citation. A bronze palm with an 'L' for Leopold monogram indicates a citation by the Minister of National Defence. On the acquisition of five of the aforementioned bronze emblems, a silver one was to be substituted in its place. On the award of five silver palms, they were then replaced by one gilt palm. In the case of civilians, the use of a bronze crenellated tower was employed. This was instigated on 23 August 1943.

Reverse Croix de Guerre 1940-1945 (BE.D028 (Spink & Son Ltd)

BE.D029 Escapers' Cross 1940-1945 — 1944

The design of this award comprises a bronze cross with straight arms, which is known numismatically as a cross pattée. The angles between the arms of the cross are filled with rays.

The central boss comprises a shield on to which is placed the Belgian lion. The reverse is plain.

The Cross was instituted on 25 February 1944 to reward Belgians

who had shown evidence of their patriotism, who had been engaged in covert work in occupied territories, had escaped from those occupied territories or had carried on clandestine work in, or escaped from, Germany itself. The award was authorized and brought into being by the Belgian government in exile in London.

The upper arm of the Cross has a metal ring attached, through which passes a 37 mm green ribbon, with 7 mm black centre stripe and 3 mm black side stripes, inset from the edge by 6 mm.

Obverse Escapers' Cross 1940-1945 (BE.D029) (Josef Charita)

BE.D030 War Medal 1940-1945 — 1946

This Medal was instituted on 16 February 1946 and comprises, on the obverse, a design incorporating a leopard's head in a 'V' chevron. On either side is the date 1940-1945. The whole design is encompassed by a laurel wreath. The reverse again has a chevron with the dates 1940-1945 and in this case the bilingual, rather than just the French inscription, as in preceding descriptions. The inscription comprises 'MEDAILLE COMMEMORATIVE DE LA GUERRE' and the Flemish 'HERIN-NERINGS MEDAILLE VAN DEN OORLOG'. The medal is round and made of artificially darkened or patinated bronze.

The Medal was to reward those Belgians who had participated in any of the branches of her fighting machine, land, sea and air units.

To the ribbon was attached a series of emblems which I will detail and describe individually, as they represent various distinct operations and, in themselves, can be loosely deemed as add-ons or grades of the medal.

Crossed Swords These were originally to reward only those who had fought in the campaign of 1940, which was to include those members of the resistance army.

Red Cross Emblem This was to denote members who had been wounded in the course of their service for their country and takes the place of the award of a Wound Medal or Wound Badge.

Bronze Wreath This emblem denotes that the recipient was a volunteer.

Lightning Flashes This insignia, which consists of two flashes of lightning, denotes that the recipient of this emblem was an intelligence agent. This emblem I find of particular interest as most countries try to hide the identity of their intelligence officers.

Bronze Bar This emblem indicates that the recipient had been a prisoner of war.

Unit Citation Bar This was a bronze bar to reward men in a unit which had received a citation in an order of the day. The emblem had the name of the particular action placed upon it.

Crossed Anchors This emblem was to denote members of the Navy and Merchant Marine who, through their service, were entitled to the Medal for service at sea.

Ellipse In 1952 a bronze oval as an Ellipse was introduced which is, to all intents and purposes, a battle or campaign bar. It is inscribed in relief with the region or country, theatre or years in which the action occurred. This was not rendered to those units that had previously received a Bar for

Reverse War Medal 1940-1945 (BE.D030)

a citation awarded in an order of the day. Examples of inscriptions that are found on the Ellipse are 'FRANCE 1944', 'PAYS-BAS 1944', 'ALLE-MAGNE 1944-1945', 'TCHECHO-SLOVAQUIE 1945' and 'AR-DENNES 1944-1945'.

The ribbon is yellow, 37 mm wide, with 6 mm side stripes, 2 mm each of black, white and black, inset from the edge by 2 mm.

BE.D031 Medal of the Resistance Army 1940-1945 — 1946

This Medal was instituted on 16 February 1946 and comprises, as its obverse design, a half figure of a young woman looking to her right or the viewer's left, with flowing hair which falls over her left shoulder. Her right arm, with clenched fist, is angled beneath her bust. Between her

fist and the ends of her hair is situated the designer's signature, which is too small to be legible. The field of the medal in this case is flat.

The reverse of the medal has a laurel wreath with the word 'Résister' and the dates '1940-1945'. The overall finish of the medal is of artificially oxidized or patinated bronze. The top of the medal has a cast ball suspender, through which is placed the medal ring suspender to which is attached the ribbon, which is 38 mm wide and black with 3.5 mm green edge stripes and two 1 mm red stripes which are situated 5 mm apart.

Obverse Medal of the Resistance Army 1940–1945 (BE.D031)

BE.D032 Medal for Volunteers 1940-1945 — 1946

This Medal was also instituted on 16 February 1946 and comprises a round medal with a thin raised edge. Across the bottom is a line that produces a flat plinth and the line becomes the horizon, over which is a rising sun that is two-thirds visible. From this emanate rays of sunlight. A capital 'V' bisects the sun with its arms reaching the upper edge line, the design symbolically depicting the rising of victory. In front of the design is a soldier in British or Free Belgian battledress, wearing a beret

Reverse Medal for Volunteers 1940–1945 (BE.D032) (Spink & Son Ltd)

and holding a rifle with fixed bayonet, butt to the ground at the British 'at ease' position.

The reverse has the Belgian lion with 'VOLONTARIIS' above and the dates '1940-1945' below.

The medal is constructed of artificially oxidized or patinated bronze, with an integral ball suspender at the top, through which is placed a ribbon ring from which it is suspended by a ribbon 38 mm wide comprising seventeen alternate stripes, made up of nine dark blue and eight red.

BE.D033 Maritime Medal 1939-1945 — 1941

This Medal was instituted on 17 July 1941 in London, by the exiled Council of Ministers and has, as its obverse design, a Belgian rampant lion without an inscription. The reverse has the royal cypher of Leopold. The medal is round with scroll ribbons at its top and was produced in bronze.

The Medal was to reward members of the Belgian Royal Navy, Merchant Navy and fishing fleet for bravery in saving life or ships at sea and was made retroactive to 3 September 1939. This Medal could also be awarded to Belgians who were serving with the equivalent British naval or merchant marine units.

The ribbon was suspended from a ring and is 37 mm wide, sea green with three 1 mm white side stripes, positioned 3 mm apart and inset 2 mm, with crossed anchors on the ribbon.

BE.D034 Civil Decoration 1940-1945 — First Class Cross — 21 July 1944

This Cross was instituted on 21 July 1944 and comprises a Maltese Cross enamelled white, with crossed torches between the arms. The royal cypher is found at the centre on both the obverse and reverse of the cross. The metal parts of the cross, in this case, are finely gilded.

It was introduced to reward civilians for distinguished service in connection with the war or war effort. It could also be awarded in particular cases to military personnel as well as foreign nationals.

The design of the ribbon comprises a 38 mm band of golden yellow, with 6 mm tricolour edges, black being outer, yellow and red inner and a 2 mm black centre stripe.

BE.D035 Civil Decoration 1940-1945 — Second Class Cross — 21 July 1944

This Cross is identical to BE.D034, save for the fact that the metal parts, instead of being gilded, are silver.

BE.D036 Civil Decoration 1940-1945 — First Class Medal — 21 July 1944

This Medal was instituted on 21 July 1944 and also comprises a Maltese Cross but in this case, the portions between the arms are filled in and there are surmounted Burgundian twigs or ragged staffs in the form of a cross. Above the medal are flatly crossed torches. The overall colour of the medal is of gilt.

It was introduced to reward civilians for distinguished service in connection with the war or war effort. It could also be awarded in particular cases to military personnel as well as foreign nationals.

The design of the ribbon comprises a 38 mm band of golden yellow, with 6 mm tricolour edges, black being outer, yellow and red inner and a 2 mm black centre stripe.

BE.D037 Civil Decoration 1940-1945 — Second Class Medal — 21 July 1944

This Medal was instituted on 21 July 1944 and is of a similar design to BE.D036, but in this case the colour is silver.

It was introduced to reward civilians for distinguished service in connection with the war or war effort. It could also be awarded in particular cases to military personnel as well as foreign nationals.

The ribbon is the same as for the First Class Medal.

BE.D038 Civil Decoration 1940-1945 — Third Class Medal — 21 July 1944

This Medal was also instituted on 21 July 1944 and is of a similar design to BE.D037, but in this case the colour of the medal is bronze. The criteria and ribbon are the same.

Obverse Civil Decoration 1940–1945 Third Class Medal (BE.D038) (Josef Charita)

BE.D039 Cross for Political Prisoners 1940-1945 — 13 November 1947

This Cross was instituted on 13 November 1947 and comprises a silver Victoria Cross with, on the obverse, a red triangle that points downwards with a black capital 'B'. The reverse has the dates '1940-1945' in black. Between the arms of the cross, in their angles, show strands of barbed wire.

Reverse Cross for Political Prisoners 1940-1945 (BE.D039) (Josef Charita)

There are narrow Bars that were awarded with the Cross, each with up to four silver stars upon it, one star emblematically to represent six months of imprisonment. These Bars are worn on the ribbon.

The design of the ribbon, which is 38 mm wide, is in thirteen equal alternate stripes, seven of white and six mid-blue.

BE.D040 Medal for Prisoners of War 1940-1945 — 1 October 1947

This Medal was instituted on 1 October 1947 and comprises a circular medal with a raised outer edge. This has a row of pellets that run round that edge up to the position of 12 o'clock, where the pommel of a short sword is situated, and round to 6 o'clock, where the blade breaks the edge. There are approximately 120 pellets that make up the design running round the edge. The short sword which constitutes the central design has downswept quillons and eight rings which go to make up the handle of the sword. This surmounts a Balkan Cross with raised edge and inner lining of pellets. On either side of the sword blade are the dates 1940 and 1945. The angles of the crosses have two pencil point rays. Around the whole of this design runs a circle of barbed wire with three barbs on either side of the sword.

The reverse has, again, a design of barbed wire with the addition of a prisoner's chain. Above the sword at the edge of the medal, is a pivot that attaches to an open work crown through which, at its top, runs a ring for attachment to the ribbon. The whole of the medal and crown is

Obverse Medal for Prisoners 1940–1945 (BE.D040) variation of design without pellets

constructed in artificially oxidized or patinated bronze.

The ribbon is black, 38 mm wide, with three 1 mm stripes at each side of red, yellow, red, situated 1 mm apart and inset 2 mm from the ribbon's edge.

BE.D041 Medal for Civil Resistance 1940-1945 — 12 February 1951

This Medal was instituted on 12 February 1951 and comprises an obverse design that depicts a half length figure of a man breaking his chains in a pose that represents resistance. A woman stands behind him, while he looks to the left, emblematically to represent the female support both tacit and actual to the resistance cause.

The reverse is inscribed with the word 'RESISTERUNT', which translates as 'They resisted', which is situated between the dates 1940-1945.

The ribbon is green, 37 mm wide, with 5 mm black edges and two 1 mm red stripes set 5 mm apart.

BE.D042 Medal for Refractories 1940-1945 — 12 February 1951

This Medal was also instituted on 12 February 1951 and comprises an obverse design that consists of a bust of a man with his arms folded in a defiant posture, looking to the right.

The reverse has the dates 1940-1945 and beneath the inscription 'FORSAN VICTI NUNQUAM SERVI', which translates as 'Vanquished perhaps, never enslaved'. The overall colour of the medal is of artificially oxidized or patinated bronze.

The Medal was to reward those Belgians who had avoided forced labour or military service that might have been imposed upon them by either the Germans or the collaborative government. The Belgian government in London had evaluated the problem of collaboration since 1942 but when liberation came, it encountered 70,000 suspects rounded up by the resistance. Subsequently 65,000 people were charged with having been members of various German or pro-German armed formations. How many more tacitly collaborated is a matter of conjecture but it must have been considerably more. 4,170 people were, in fact, sentenced to death, of whom 3,193 had been convicted of military collaboration; however only 230 executions were carried out at the Belgian Army camp at Beverloo.

It is interesting to note that the colour combination of the ribbon of this Medal changes to represent varying grades of award. Thus, the two 3 mm stripes that are positioned 11 mm apart in yellow, represent Belgians who in May 1940 refused to honour any military duties imposed by the Germans or collaborative government. White represents refusal to undertake work for the Germans. Red represents those who had, before 6 June 1944, returned to Belgium on leave, having submitted to a deportation order for forced labour in Germany and had deserted and avoided return to Germany. Taking into account the size of collaboration already illustrated in Belgium, the award of this Medal shows no mean endeavour to one's convictions.

The ribbon is thus 37 mm wide and of a green colour, with two 3 mm stripes situated 11 mm apart from one of the preceding colours.

Reverse Medal for Refractories 1940-1945 (BE.D042) (Josef Charita)

BE.D043 Medal of Belgian Gratitude 1940-1945 — Gold — 1 August 1945
BE.D044 Medal of Belgian Gratitude 1940-1945 — Silver — 1 August 1945
BE.D045 Medal of Belgian Gratitude 1940-1945 — Bronze — 1 August 1945

This Medal was instituted on 1 August 1945 and is octagonal in shape, its height being wider than its breadth, measuring 36 mm long by 32 mm wide. The obverse design has a female head to represent Belgium, which is situated on the left of the medal. The female head is veiled and looking to her right. In her hand, she holds upright in salute an antique sword. This represents recognition. Above the body of the medal is a small laurel wreath. In the case of the

award being rendered for Red Cross work, there is a small red enamelled cross in the normal void of the wreath. It is possible to find examples with the red cross not enamelled and this gives rise to two cases of speculation. The first is that they were not enamelled for reasons of economy, or they were left unenamelled for those who were not entitled to the Red Cross type, to save the manufacturer the cost of two dies. My inclination is to follow the first principle as it would be an easy matter for a manufacturer to cut out the cross as a separate step in the manufacturing process, which in itself would not significantly increase the cost of production.

The reverse has the inscription 'PATRIA GRATIA' which translates as 'Thanks of the Fatherland'.

The medal was to reward both Belgians and foreigners for acts of heroism, courage or deeds of a humanitarian, charitable or philanthropic nature and Red Cross work which was occasioned in connection with the war.

The medal is found in three colours, gold, silver and bronze, the colour of the individual grades representing the various degrees of indebtedness of the nation to the recipient.

The ribbon is 37 mm wide and violet in colour, with a 6 mm central stripe of the Belgian national colours,

that is to say 2 mm of black, 2 mm yellow and 2 mm red.

Obverse Medal of Belgian Gratitude 1940-1945 Bronze (BE.D045) (Josef Charita)

BE.D046 Abyssinian Campaign Medal 1941 — 30 January 1947

This Medal was instituted on 30 January 1947 and is trapezoidal in shape with two sides incurved. The medal is again higher than it is wide, being 45 mm tall by 31 mm wide. The base is inset approximately by 2 mm and the top is flat on to which is an oblong box with a raised eyelet, through which runs the medal ribbon ring. The base is curved up at each end and slightly higher than the body of the trapezoid. This has a raised edge that follows the medal and is as

wide as the base is set back. The ensuing field is concave, on to which are positioned the heads of two soldiers. The one in the foreground is negroid with open-necked shirt and wearing a fez type hat with neck flap and chin strap under his chin. The soldier in the background is Arab in features, or could be interpreted as a white colonial with, again, open-necked shirt and wearing a topee. They look to their left, the viewer's right. From the junction of the fez with the outer line runs a spray of laurel leaves, which finishes halfway down the opposite side of the medal. On the base are the dates 1940-1941.

The reverse has inscribed upon it the names of the campaigns and actions to which the medal pertains, namely 'SAYO', 'GAMBELLA' and 'ASOSA'. The medal is of artificially oxidized or patinated bronze. It was awarded to Belgian officers and men in Abyssinia between 6 March and 3 July 1941 and commemorates their loyal service to the country.

The design of the ribbon is of five stripes of green, blue, yellow, blue, green, the central stripe being 5 mm wide and the others 8 mm. The total overall width of the ribbon is 37 mm. One Bar was issued for wear on the ribbon; produced in bronze, it has the inscription 'ABYSSINIE'.

Obverse Abyssinian Campaign Medal 1941 (BE.D046) (Josef Charita)

BE.D047 African War Medal 1940-1945 — 30 January 1947

This Medal was introduced on 30 January 1947 and produced in bronze with, again, a unique design that comprises a curved-based medal, with straight sides. These rise and produce shoulders which then rise again parallel to the sides, terminating in a flat top. This has a further outer edge that runs from approximately 5 mm from the bottom and follows the line of the medal. There is a concave panel with semi-circular top and bottom, into which are two similar soldiers in profile facing to the right, the viewer's left. Unlike BE.D046, the profiles are full. The

negro is in the foreground and the Arab, in this case, has taken on more European features. The negro wears the fez type hat with neckcloth and chinstrap under his chin, while the European wears the topee.

The base panel that is formed by the semi-circular bottom of the medal and panel, has the date 1940-1945 encased, following the line of the top and bottom of the panel. The reverse of the medal is plain.

This Medal was to reward officers and other ranks who, between 19 May 1940 and 7 May 1945, had served for a period of not less than one year, or had sustained a wound or been killed in action, when the award was rendered to the next of kin, or had been decorated or Mentioned in Despatches. The actual campaigns were indicated by the award of a campaign Bar, of which four were authorized. Albeit only one applies to this work, I have included them all for completeness as they will be encountered often on this medal and it will be more correct to cover them here than to have the medal described in two volumes of the series. Thus the Bars are 'NIGERIE', 'MOYEN-ORIENT', 'MADAGASCAR' and 'BIRMANIE'.

The qualification period was differ-ent for each Bar and was six months for the Middle East, which is the only relevant Bar, which encompassed Egypt, Palestine, Tripolitania, Sudan and North Africa. It was three months' service for Nigeria and Burma and one month for Madagas-car, all of these being outside the scope of the defined areas that this book covers. Foreign personnel who had assisted the Belgian forces in a capacity of liaison officers received the Medal without a Bar.

The ribbon is of pale blue and measures 37 mm wide, with a yellow centre stripe and side stripes that are inset by 6 mm of yellow which, in this case, are 2.5 mm wide.

BE.D048 Medal of the Military Fighters of the 1940-1945 War — 16 December 1967

This Medal was belatedly introduced on 16 December 1967 and consists of a square armed cross with a raised edge. The angles have semi-circles in them, giving an impression of the cross surmounting a round medal. These semi-circles have a raised edge as well. The field of both the cross and the semi-circles is pebbled upwards as the central design is a double-edged sword with a disproportionately broad tip. On either side of the blade are positioned the dates 1940 and 1945. The upper arm has a ball finial with chamfered top and bottom through which runs the ribbon ring. The reverse of the cross has the Belgian rampant lion. The medal is constructed of bronze and is 37 mm by 37 mm, but collectors will encoun-

Reverse Medal of the Military Fighters of the 1940-1945 War (BE.D048) (Josef Charita)

ter variations in design and size and this should not be considered extraordinary, because in excess of ten firms are known to have produced the Medal from individual designs taken from a very poor drawing of the official design.

The Medal was intended to reward members of both Belgian and foreign fighting forces who had served in an active duty capacity, with the exiled Belgian forces or free Belgian forces who were stationed or raised in Great Britain.

The design of the ribbon, which is again 37 mm wide, has an 11 mm yellow centre flanked by narrow black, yellow and red stripes. The total measurement of these three is 7 mm, with a bright green edge which measures 6 mm.

Belgian Flying Wings
BE.A001 Officer Pilots' Wings — October 1935-1946

This badge was introduced in October 1935 upon the accession of King Leopold III and continued in use until 1946. The badge comprises a cloth backing of either black or grey wool cloth, on to which is embroidered a pair of wings. Between the wings are a pair of 'L's for Leopold in diagonal gold wire, with a Roman III between, again worked in diagonal wire embroidery. The 'L's are tilted forwards and face each other. Each wing is made up of seven rows of fletching which is constructed of overlapping gold sequins. The holes in the sequins, where they are attached to the cloth backing, form a central line on each row and are again worked in gold wire. The inner fletching and wing joint that made the frame for the 'L's is again gold-embroidered and is executed on the opposite diagonal to that employed on the 'L's.

The whole design is surmounted by the Belgian Crown which is worked in bullion, the inner part of the crown being worked over red silk. The overall measurements of the badge are 112 mm across by 35 mm high.

The badge was worn on the left shoulder of the Belgian uniform, approximately six inches (150 mm) down the sleeve. There were two basic uniforms for the Belgian Air Force, being at this time but a branch of the Army. The first uniform was khaki and of the same style employed by the Army; the second, introduced in 1930, was a blue-grey uniform. However, with the defeat of Belgium,

Officer Pilots' Wings (BE.A001) (A. Forman)

their air personnel were integrated into the RAF. On 12 February 1942, the Belgian Air Force was reborn in England and thenceforth wore RAF uniform which had only the Belgian nationality title on the arms. They served mainly in 349 and 350 squadrons. In these cases they were entitled to British Pilots' Wings (GB.A001) which they wore on the right breast and the Belgian Pilots' Wings were worn on the left.

BE.A002 NCO Pilots' Wings — October 1935-1946

This badge, to all intents and purposes, is identical to the former Officer Pilots' Wings (BE.A001) and I will leave the reader to substitute silver for gold in the text. The method of wear and historical background for the use on RAF uniform is also identical to that described formerly.

BE.A003 Other Ranks Pilots' Wings — October 1935-1946

This badge was also introduced in October 1935 but in this case was produced in bronze metal rather than bullion. The design is identical but the fletching of the wings is narrower. The area between the wings and the tilted 'L's is voided, while the area between the 'L's and the Roman III is filled in.

This badge was worn by Corporals and Privates on the right breast of their tunic. It is highly improbable that this badge would be worn on the RAF tunic as all pilots were mustered as Sergeant Pilots or above in rank. Thus, it can be confidently stated that this badge was a purely Belgian award. However, I feel sure that some photograph will prove me wrong in this assumption!

BE.A004 Officer Observers' Badge — October 1935-1946

This badge was also introduced in October 1935 and comprises an identical design to the Pilot Officers' Wings (BE.A001), save that the left-hand set of fletching, or wing, is not attached. There are also examples with the right-hand part of the wing not present. The measurement of either example is 66 mm horizontally and 35 mm vertically. They were worn on the sleeve.

BE.A005 NCO Observers' Badge — October 1935-1946

This badge was also introduced in October 1935 and is identical in design to the NCO Pilots' Wings (BE.A002) save that the left-hand wing is missing. It is also finished in silver. There is an example of this wing with the opposite hand fletching missing also.

BE.A006 Other Ranks Observers' Badge — October 1935-1946

This badge was produced in bronze metal and worn on the right breast of the Belgian uniform by Corporals and below and took the same basic design as the Other Ranks Pilots' Wings (BE.A003). It is highly improbable that this badge was worn on the British uniform as observers usually were made up to the rank of Sergeant in the Royal Air Force.

BE.A007 Flying Personnel Student Officers' Badge — October 1935-1946

This set of wings comprises a half wing constructed in metal which was then gilded. It takes the form of the Other Ranks Observers' Badge (BE.A006) and, like that badge, was worn on the right breast of the uniform. This, again, would not be used on the British uniform as the student officer would be commissioned and then receive the full wings that were applicable to the examination that he had passed.

BE.A008 Flying Personnel Student NCOs' Badge — October 1935-1946

This badge consists of a metal half wing which is identical to the officers' type (BE.A007) but, in this case, it is finished in silver. The badge was worn on the right breast of the uniform but it would be highly unlikely to have been worn on the British uniform for the same reasons as the two previous badges, BE.A006 and BE.A007.

Index of Awards

French Awards

Norwegian Awards

Index of people, units and relevant items